Negotiation Rules!

Here's to your negotiation success! Jeanette Nyden

You can't play a game if you don't know the rules. Jeanette Nyden's new book provides a handy summary of exactly what the rules are in negotiation. Featuring a survey of both win-win and competitive tactics, it presents readers with a straightforward, comprehensive planning system they can use the day they buy the book.

Professor G. Richard Shell, author of *Bargaining for Advantage* and *The Art of Woo*, and director of the Wharton Executive Negotiation Workshop.

Negotiation Rules! A Practical Approach to Big Deal Negotiations skillfully and positively presents the essentials of negotiating. The clear and sensible approach to negotiation strategy is indispensable. The importance of perspective, patience and a willingness to engage, even if I don't love the process, has helped me personally, professionally and our company immeasurably.

Brian Cummings, President Alumco, Inc.

If you are a business professional, grab this book... study it...and implement its teachings. Jeanette Nyden shows you the way to mastering tough negotiations. Her negotiation techniques are subtle, yet powerful...so pay close attention!"

Lee B. Salz, CEO of Business Expert Webinars, President of Sales Architects, and author of the award-winning book *Soar Despite Your Dodo Sales Manager*

Praise for Negotiation Rules

Jeanette Nyden has succinctly set forth the most important lessons in the art of negotiation for busy professionals who seek increased confidence and improved skills at the bargaining table. This book distills the essence of an entire library of negotiation tips in one practical and readable package. Get it, read it, and use it right away for better negotiation results!

T. Noble Foster, MBA, JD, Assistant Professor of Business Law, Albers School of Business & Economics, Seattle University

In *Negotiation Rules!* Jeanette Nyden provides an easy to follow, systematic approach to negotiation. The framework she provides for organizing the factors that impact the outcome of a negotiation demystifies the bargaining process. The insights she provides into negotiating are universally applicable and practical. The understanding I gained from this book and Jeanette's training have helped me level the playing field when negotiating with larger, more sophisticated companies. This book is a must read for anyone who is responsible for leading or participating in a negotiation.

Kevin Moschetti, President, Esterline Palomar Products

Negotiation Rules! should be on every Sales Professional's reading list. By following the approach in this book you will close BIGGER deals, create happier customers, and ultimately bring home a bigger paycheck.

Jeb Blount, author of *Power Principles* and *Sales Guy's 7 Rules for Outselling the Recession*

Praise for Negotiation Rules

..................▶

Negotiation Rules! sets forth an intriguing model for negotiation. I know from experience that the concepts and tactics in Jeanette's book work. She has crafted them from her experience and has masterfully laid them out here. I will place this book alongside my favorite "how-to" books, the ones I turn to for expertise in life, in work and in relationships.

MaryPat Theiler-Cheng, Vice President, Netstar Communications, Inc.

Negotiation Rules!

A Practical Approach To Big Deal Negotiations

Jeanette Nyden

Cape Coral, Florida

Sales Gravy Press
The Sales Book Publisher™
1726 SE 44th Terrace
Cape Coral, Florida 33904

Published by Sales Gravy Press
Printed in the United States of America

Cover Design: Dave Blaker

First Edition

Library of Congress Control Number: 2009930226

ISBN-13: 978-0-9818004-7-9
ISBN-10: 0-9818004-7-5

Table of Contents

............................➤

"Winning is not everything but wanting to win is."

Vincent Thomas

Foreword

..............................➤

For many years, I dreaded any interaction that involved negotiations. I saw it as a stupid game, with clear winners and losers. My personal ineptness virtually guaranteed that I came out on the short end of any deal.

The first time I felt like a fool was during a college trip to Mexico. After shopping for hours in the local market, I finally decided to buy a leather jacket. When I asked how much it cost, the shop owner quoted me a price that was far less than what I'd pay in the U.S.

"I'll take it!" I said, excited to be getting such a good deal.

When I showed it to my traveling companions several hours later, one blurted out, "You got screwed. I paid half that amount."

My elation quickly evaporated as I envisioned the shop-keeper laughing at the stupid Americano who paid twice what the jacket was worth.

Several years later, my husband and I went to buy a new Honda Civic. It wasn't long before he and the dealer salesman were engaged in this ridiculous bickering about the price. At one point, my husband said, "That's my final offer."

I was appalled. I couldn't believe he was willing to walk

away, when he knew how much I wanted that car. When the salesman returned with his counteroffer, I decided it was time to get involved.

"We'll take it!" I said, looking forward to driving my new vehicle home. My husband glared at me – and later chastised me for butting in because we'd left money on the table.

As you might imagine, I had minimal confidence in my ability to negotiate. Fortunately, when I took a sales job at Xerox, they had a "no deals" policy. The price was the price, no matter who you were. I was relieved.

But, as I found out when I started my own consulting company, I couldn't avoid negotiations forever. Despite quoting a fair price for my services, some clients felt compelled to get a better deal.

When I realized that my negative perception of negotiation was impacting my success, I knew it was time to get educated on this "beast." It took awhile to accept that negotiating wasn't personal. Initially I felt awkward when negotiating, but over the years I've improved.

The hardest part for me still is when I really, really want something to happen. I get that "backed into the corner" feeling that immediately positions me in a one-down position when trying to reach agreement. Maybe you know what I mean!

Several years ago, I had a unique opportunity with an e-learning company that wanted to feature my work as a sales expert. But their complex contract was filled with legal mumbo jumbo with potentially long-ranging ramifications for my intellectual property.

That's when I contacted attorney Jeanette Nyden to represent me. I was immediately impressed with her mastery of the negotiation process as she coached me into reaching a satisfactory deal.

Knowing I'm not alone with my negotiation angst, I urged her to make her expertise available to all the business executives, salespeople and entrepreneurs who need help in this area. I'm so glad she finally wrote *Negotiation Rules!*

If you lack confidence in your ability to negotiate, this book shows you how to reframe the process so it's not a win-lose proposition. If you're an experienced negotiator, you'll discover how to take your skills to the next level.

Some of my favorite takeaways from *Negotiation Rules!* include the strategies on how to:

Deal with power imbalances. You'll find out how to recognize your own power and level the playing field ¬ even when you're dealing with bigger companies or large opportunities.

Engage in fruitful dialogue. You'll learn questions you can use to uncover motivations, focus on what really matters, ensure collaboration and keep the process moving forward.

Set the negotiation "anchor." You'll discover how to establish the point around which the entire negotiation process revolves.

Effectively prepare for discussions. Winging it just doesn't work if you want a successful agreement. When you're prepared, your negotiated results are substantially better.

Transform demands for price concession. You'll find new options for those always-stressful situations that can make or break a potential deal.

Negotiation Rules! takes the mystique out of negotiations and replaces it with mastery. When you study Nyden's clearly defined process and leverage the tools she provides, you're guaranteed a much better outcome than you could have imagined.

Personally, I no longer fear negotiations. I realize it's simply a part of doing business that actually involves a great deal of creativity – especially when approached from a "How can we make this work for both us?" perspective. You can have that self-assurance too! Just keep reading ...

Jill Konrath
Author, *Selling to Big Companies*
CEO, SellingtoBigCompanies.com

Introduction

··················▶

Have you ever wondered, "What do successful negotiators know, say, do or think that gets them great results? Why are they more at ease and have more confidence?" Successful negotiators are easy to spot because they appear deliberate, authoritative and authentic at the bargaining table. And, they consistently negotiate great deals.

If you're not satisfied with the deals that you negotiate, you should improve your negotiation skills. Many business people love the thrill of the hunt, but they don't like the thrill of the negotiations to close that deal! You don't have to suffer through stressful negotiations just to get a mediocre deal. You can, and must, negotiate great deals.

Negotiation Success Leave Clues

This book offers you a systematic approach to negotiating that will show you what successful negotiators know, do and think. By examining common negotiation principles and real life success stories, bargaining will be more transparent, and less mysterious. At the end of the day, all that matters is the quality of the deal you close.

Develop the skills and confidence you need to successfully negotiate any deal in today's economy.

Learn to:

- Uncover hidden agendas that could derail your deal
- Effectively negotiate price without sacrificing your bottom line
- Demand and define trade offs that help get a balanced deal
- Know when to make concessions and when to demand a trade off
- Use influence to sway your counterpart to see things your way
- Manage power imbalances between you and your counterpart

Improved skills lead to enhanced confidence, which naturally leads to better negotiated outcomes. This has been my experience for many years. Here are some of the results that you can expect after applying the suggestions in this book.

- More ease during potentially stressful negotiations
- More confidence that you are making the right choices, reading the situation the right way, and doing what's right at any given moment
- More comfort with your performance at the bargaining table, the process itself and your relationship with your counterpart
- More trust in the back-and-forth nature of the negotiation process
- More flexibility and self reliance

If you'd like to achieve this level of ease, the tips, techniques and strategies outlined in this book are for you.

Today's Frustrations

Business people tell me that they are frustrated with their deals. In particular, business people complain about giving in, making unilateral concessions, and misunderstanding their role at the bargaining table. If these folks are not satisfied with the deal, it is likely that their counterparts may not be happy either.

Business people also report changes at the bargaining table that they are not prepared for. Technologies like reverse on-line auctions and email have changed the way we do business and how we negotiate. As budgets get tighter, people are asked to do more with less. What does that mean to the contracts you negotiate?

The Solution

Business people who negotiate any kind of business to business agreements will benefit from this book. The principles discussed throughout this book will help you see negotiations from a different perspective, validate some of what you already know, and help you get some quick tips that can be easily applied at your next negotiation.

This book can be studied by reading chapters in sequential order or by reading only those chapters that seem to apply to your present negotiation. My aim in placing the chapters in their particular order is to allow the reader to have a comprehensive, step-by-step plan for approaching all forms of business negotiations. In other words, you can only appreciate the significance of normative leverage after grasping the concept of interest based negotiation.

My Story

I haven't always been a great negotiator. In fact, I've made some pretty big blunders in my career. The negotiation that still stings me with regret happened about ten years ago. At that time, I was a trial lawyer negotiating with a managing partner at a Chicago law firm for my salary and benefits. I'd been practicing for seven years and knew enough to know that I did not have enough information to have the discussion.

In response to his question about my salary requirements I said, "I'm not prepared to negotiate my salary." Good, right? Wrong. Ten minutes later I was negotiating my salary and benefits! And, my numbers were so low that when he called to offer me the job, he offered me $5,000 more per year in starting salary. Do you have any idea how much money I'd left on the table if the managing partner at a law firm is willing to pay you more than your asking price? How about $20,000! That is my rough estimate based on what my colleagues were making at their firms. That's not my only negotiation blunder; it is just the one that still smarts after all these years.

How did this happen? How did I end up negotiating against myself when I said I wouldn't? How did any of the mistakes that I made happen? I'm a lot like other negotiators. I've been humiliated, frustrated, boxed into a corner, and left out of conversations. I've experienced all of the same emotions too, fear, frustration and nagging doubts. Something triggered me to look at what other negotiators were doing that seemed to get them great outcomes. One day it all came together.

Co-counsel and I developed this strategy for negotiating with our opponent. I was the bad cop—no surprises there! I was going to pound the other guy with my superior knowledge and trial skills—I'm not kidding—to scare him into being reasonable with my co-counsel. Well, if this sounds like a ridiculous tactic, you are correct. About five minutes into the negotiations I had an epiphany. I suddenly saw things from my counterpart's perspective. I don't mean the facts of the case, but all of the political and economic circumstances driving his position. At that moment, I changed tactics—without letting co-counsel know—and reached out to lay the foundation for common ground. Everyone wanted this contentious, wasteful case over with. I pitched a risky settlement offer. I didn't even know if my client would accept it, but I did think that my counterpart could live with it. Two months later, the case settled.

That one experience drastically changed the course of my career. Three years after that settlement, I was trained as a mediator. I've spent hundreds of hours over the last six years mediating cases, including business disputes and disputes at the grassroots level. I've also worked with hundreds of business people to improve both their confidence and skill level at the bargaining table. This whole time, I've kept in mind what it means to leverage common ground and what that can do to any relationship, including business to business relationships.

The stories I re-tell in this book are mainly from my experiences as a negotiation coach and trainer. But, I also draw on my experiences as a professional mediator. When I'm mediating, I am facilitating negotiations between two or more parties who cannot seem to reach an agreement on their own. Because as a mediator I must remain completely neutral, I've learned to look at the negotiations differently. I've learned to clearly see the merits of both sides to any situation. That ability has shaped my perspective as a negotiation a coach and trainer. I no longer focus only on one side of the story. I am much more able to understand what may motivate someone else and what types of leverage they might respond to, for example. I challenge my coaching and training clients to do the same.

I encourage you to challenge all of your assumptions as you read this book. I find that circumstances that lead to impasse can be easily overcome by examining our assumptions and clarifying the assumptions of our counterparts. I also encourage you to share your thoughts from reading this book with colleagues. My mission is to bring greater harmony and understanding to business to business negotiations. I want people to shift their perspective from one of competition and positions to one of collaboration and common ground, and I can only do that by spreading the word.

I wish you well at your next negotiation.

Jeanette Nyden

Chapter One

....►

What Does Interest Based Negotiating Mean?

Interest based negotiating is a term of art used to explain the fact that people have positive reasons for the positions they take at the bargaining table. That simple. The theory goes like this: If you can unearth and understand your counterpart's interests at the bargaining table, you will reach an agreement.

Difficult Concept in Practice

In practice, the idea that your counterpart has a positive reason for hammering you to make a price concession can be difficult to understand in the heat of the moment. More importantly, people in the business world don't ever use the word interests as part of their jargon. People do talk about their positions. They know their counterpart's positions. They also talk about the position that they will take refuting their counterpart's position, and so goes the conversation.

Explaining the concept of interest based negotiating has been my daily activity for the last six years. I intuitively understood this concept after my stint as a volunteer mediator at a community mediation center. My coaching and training clients though, didn't quickly grasp the concept and some had a real hard time accepting it. In fact, the more that someone had been in contentious negotiations, the less likely they thought that their counterpart had any positive interests, just ridiculous positions.

The Next Step

Understanding negotiation interests is a challenge because we talk more openly in business about drivers and motivations than we do about interests. The term interests has a subtle connotation, which can be confusing to some. People think of interests in terms of what interests them, like what books they like or what movies they like. The term motivation, on the other hand, seems to resonate better with my clients, and I therefore, use the terms motivations and interests interchangeably throughout this book to make my points.

It is now time to take the next step if we are to achieve our desire for greater understanding and collaboration in business to business negotiations. I've designed this book for you to explore negotiation principles from the point of view that everyone comes to the bargaining table with positive, motivators for doing business with you. All stages of negotiating, from setting goals, selecting and countering tactics, to formulating a strategy are outlined from the perspective of how to leverage common ground for maximum gain.

As you read individual chapters keep in mind that it is by understanding our positive motivations and those of our counterpart that we reach mutually beneficial agreements. My firm belief is this: By leveraging shared interests you find common ground. By finding common ground you reach an agreement.

Getting to Yes and Getting Past No

Getting to Yes: Negotiating Agreement Without Giving In[1] is the book that broke a lot of valuable ground, and it is still taught today as the foundation for negotiation and mediation courses all over the country. *Getting to Yes* sets the stage for distinguishing between one's negotiation position and one's interests.

Approximately ten years later, William Ury, the co-author of *Getting to Yes*, published an even better book, *Getting Past No: Negotiating Your Way from Confrontation to Cooperation*. [2] This book really explains how to use interest based negotiating in your everyday dealings with people. I, therefore, pay homage to those that came before me and who dramatically influenced my view of collaborative negotiations. This book is entirely based on the principle of interest based negotiations. My mission is to make that concept accessible for all those business people who negotiate as part of their duties and who can benefit from leveraging this concept.

Chapter Two

································▶

Uncovering Hidden Motivations

Motivations dominate the negotiation process. Negotiators knowingly chose or unwittingly react based on their motivations. Motivations can be overt, like purchasing your product at the lowest possible price, or less obvious, like wanting to use your services simply because your company works with a prestigious Fortune 500 company. Motivations can also be intentionally obscured from your counterpart, or hidden from yourself due to a lack of introspection.

Hidden motivations can derail the most well meaning negotiators, sidetrack an otherwise focused bargaining session, and create avoidable obstacles to agreement.

Successful negotiators spend more time trying to uncover the other party's motivations.

Professor Leigh Thompson analyzed 5,000 negotiations and found something astounding: Negotiators discovered shared interests only 50% of the time.[1] Those are the same odds as flipping a coin. Hidden motivations were the culprit. Negotiators were either bluffing or they were imprecise in talking about their own interests, thus preventing them from recognizing when motivations were shared. Without a clear understanding of the motivations at play you are less likely to negotiate a mutually beneficial arrangement.

Successful negotiators know two important things: What is motivating them and what is likely motivating their counterpart to make a deal. They also understand that information is power. Therefore, they assume that all negotiators have hidden agendas.

Recognizing hidden agendas will most significantly help you strike better deals at the bargaining table. Just because your counterpart is bluffing, or vague about her/his motivations doesn't mean that you have to remain in the dark. You can develop the ability to distinguish between stated positions and true motivations. You must be willing to acknowledge that most of your counterpart's motivations are legitimate from their point of view. You must also be willing to discuss motivations and move the conversation away from a position of tit-for-tat. This chapter will enable you to distinguish between positions and interests at the bargaining table. Once you have this ability, you will recognize ways to trade and leverage interests into an agreement.

Negotiation Defined

"Negotiation is the back and forth communication aimed at reaching agreement with others when some of your interests are shared and some are opposed."[2] There are four distinct parts:

- Back and forth communication
- Aimed at reaching an agreement
- Some interests are shared
- Some interests are opposed

From my perspective interests are the same as motivations at the bargaining table. A negotiation interest can be elusive, even for those who negotiate for a living, precisely because negotiators are trained to take positions.

Two Problems with Positions

A position is a stance that you take at the bargaining table. It is the "what" at the bargaining table. It answers the question, *what do we want?* Negotiators are more comfortable talking about their positions, and for good reason. A position stabilizes the negotiator and appears to give the negotiation some meaning or direction. Negotiators are not as comfortable talking about the "why" behind the position. For this reason, positions often intentionally obscure legitimate interests and create hidden agendas.

At the bargaining table, and in planning sessions, I often hear things like, "our position is . . ." or "they took the position that. . . ." In fact, American media, television shows, movies and commentators all portray position taking as the gold standard for admirable negotiators. Listen very carefully and you too will recognize positions. "Our townspeople deserve justice for this crime." "You are with us or you are against us." "That costs too much."

> **Positions send a signal to the other party that you are not willing to engage in a back and forth dialogue to reach an agreement.**

Signal an unwillingness to negotiate. Positions are inflexible, immutable stakes in the sand. Positions send a signal to the other party that you are unwilling to engage in a back and forth dialogue to reach an agreement. Remember that back and forth communication is at the very heart of what it means to negotiate. If you signal an unwillingness to engage in a back and forth conversation, you are not negotiating. You are battling for supremacy.

For a more visual image, imagine that each time you, a colleague or your opponent at the bargaining table speak in terms of your positions you are holding up a stop sign, thereby indicating an unwillingness to listen to one another. Position taking makes engaging in back and forth conversation very difficult until one person makes a concerted effort to get past his or her position.

Focus attention away from what really matters. Positions are quite literally the tip of the iceberg. We recognize positions from a mile away just like sailors see the tip of an iceberg from a great distance. The problem for the sailor and the negotiator is how to determine the depth and breadth of that iceberg. In both nature and at the bargaining table, nine times as much mass lies beneath the waterline as floats above the waterline. Just as a majority of the iceberg is obscured beneath the waterline, our motivations are equally obscured from view. If you focus all of your attention on the tip of the iceberg (your counterpart's positions) you will miss shared interests and miscalculate the depth and breadth of your counterpart's motivations. As icebergs cause terrible damage to ships that have the unfortunate circumstance to come into contact with them, you too, run the risk of hitting the metaphorical iceberg and sinking your negotiation ship.

Your success as a negotiator depends on your ability to look beyond positions, uncover hidden interests, and leverage shared interests.

Interests are the Cornerstone

Your success as a negotiator depends on your ability to look beyond positions, uncover hidden interests, and leverage shared interests. The problem is that very few good negotiators openly discuss interests and most average negotiators don't even know what their interests are, let alone use them as a cornerstone upon which to build a solid foundation. Interests are your motivations for the position you take. They are, therefore, the cornerstone at each and every negotiation. When negotiators take a position, they are actually protecting an underlying interest.

Unearthing Motivations. The first step in any negotiation is to identify your own interests. Without a clear understanding of your own motivations you cannot use your leverage, manage the other side's tactics or overcome an impasse. To begin identifying interests list all the reasons why you want to take a position. Here are some questions that will help you uncover your motivations.

- How will this agreement benefit you or your company?
- What is the most important thing you need from your counterpart to make this agreement reasonable from your perspective?
- What one or two things will derail this deal?
- What's so important about getting a deal or agreement from this person or company, as opposed to someone else?
- What do you have that your counterpart wants, needs or cannot live without?

The next step would be to identify your counterpart's possible hidden motivations. While many people report being able to identify their own interests, they draw a complete blank at identifying the other person's motivations. Because we can become so enamored with our own positions, we see someone else's position as a threat to our interests. This barrier prevents us from contemplating a differing point of view. Once we step into another's shoes, we are able to see that their position might just be motivated by some important interests. Uncovering the other party's interests might be difficult, but it is a key to your success.

A colleague of mine took told me a story about a confrontation with her boss. When her boss told her she had to attend a team meeting, my colleague told her boss, "I'm not going. These meetings waste my time!" That is clearly a position because it does not indicate at all what motivated her to take that stance. As a negotiator, if you faced this position could you uncover the hidden motivations and find common ground to reach an agreement? It is your job as a skilled negotiator to ask yourself some questions that will lead to a clearer understanding of those hidden interests. Here are some ways to do that.

First, you will need to step into her shoes. Can you imagine a scenario which would prompt someone to say something like that? Can you imagine what makes her "feel" that way? If you can truly look at an issue from the speaker's point of view, you can often catch a glimpse of what might be motivating them to take a position. I put myself in her shoes to imagine what would force her to say that, and, as a result, I asked the question, "What made you say that?"

My colleague responded this way, "Well, the systems engineers were supposed to have payroll software upgrade integrated by now, and it is not. We've been in 2 hour long meetings at least once a week for 3 months now talking about the integration. My work load just keeps growing, and I am working Saturdays just to be able to get my part of payroll done every two weeks. My boss says that he will not authorize anymore overtime. How am I supposed to get everything done if I have to sit through another 2 hour meeting this week? I am so frustrated right now."

Hearing this response, if her boss were a good negotiator, she would be able to parse out several hidden motivations. Then using these motivations, she would then make some offers that met her employee's needs while also meeting the department's needs. Some motivations might be:

- Getting work done in the usual 40 hour work week.
- Being paid for overtime hours.
- Getting the upgrade integrated and working without her involvement in meetings.

Taking this analysis one step further, one might also detect resentment and a lack of understanding of her contributions at the meetings. Or, going out on a limb, maybe there is no good reason to have her at the meetings. Maybe her boss takes the position that she must attend, but has not looked at her role at the meetings, the impact that the meetings are having on her workload, and whether there is another solution other than having her attend the meetings. Once you have begun to indentify interests, you will start to see the complexity that positions hide.

Colleague's Position	Possible Motivations
"I'm not going. These meetings waste my time!"	• Getting work done in the usual 40 hour work week. • Being paid for overtime hours. • Getting the upgrade integrated and working without her involvement in meetings. • Unclear understanding of her role at the meetings.

Interests Can Be Traded. Interests, unlike positions, can be used like a currency to make exchanges. My colleague's boss could trade allowing my colleague to miss the meeting in exchange for no more overtime on Saturdays. Or, she could trade an email check-in to the team lead in exchange for in-person attendance at the meeting. There might be many more solutions. Once you've identified the hidden interests, you will also find common ground.

Interests Are *Always* Positive. Interests are always positive from the speaker's perspective. This can be a tough concept to swallow because from our point of view, many times their positions seem to conflict with our motivations, and therefore, must be wrong. Using this concept as a lens through which to view your counterpart's positions, you might find yourself understanding their motivations, even those that are in direct opposition to your own. To do this successfully, you must truly look at an issue from the speaker's point of view — without judgment or criticism.

Let me tell you about the day that I learned that first hand interests are always positive from the speaker's point of view. At the time, I was a volunteer mediator-in-training at the King County Dispute Resolution Center in Seattle, Washington. The KCDRC required all mediators to attend free 2 hour advanced training sessions. I attended a session about helping mediators learn to identify the interests behind positions. We all took turns guessing at the interests underlying positions like, "My God won't let me agree to that." After more than an hour, I was incredulous at best that there could ever be any positive motivations underlying these bizarre positions. Then the instructor put a Denis Rodman quote from the newspaper on the board and asked if anyone knew the positive underlying interest. I instantly knew: He wanted autonomy. I triumphantly announced that autonomy was Rodman's underlying interest.

The woman to my left, also an attorney, asked, "Since when is autonomy a positive interest?" We looked at each other in disbelief. I was about to start my own company because I felt claustrophobic in a traditional firm setting. Autonomy was everything to me. As someone who had thrived in a traditional law firm, my friend did not see autonomy as a positive interest, but rather as a threat to firm stability. These two motivations, autonomy and stability, appeared to be set in opposition to one another.

Once I was able to see that from the firm's point of view, hierarchy and stability has its legitimate purpose, I was far less put out by it. I was still going to start my own business, but now, I could see things from the firm's point of view. I had a glimpse at their reasons for their reactions. I also saw how confusing my actions were to them. This epiphany set me in motion on my journey of enhancing negotiation skills.

Always strive to peel the onion to look for positive interests underlying surface positions. Look beyond the immediate actions and how those actions might adversely impact you. Look at situations from the speaker's point of view.

Two Words of Caution
It is imperative that I sound a note of caution on this seemingly idealistic concept that interests are always positive. A very small percentage of the population is motivated by very ugly feelings. I recently had the displeasure of negotiating with a man who was hostile, angry and emotionally out of control. I still managed to reach a settlement with him on behalf of my client. My own sense of outrage at his bad behavior made it difficult for me to recognize his motivations. I had to literally rise above the situation and make some educated guesses about some positive interests. Nevertheless, I acted upon those educated guesses and eventually got a deal. Not everyone in the world is sane, mentally stable or congenial. As economic pressures ramp up, more and more people may

start acting in ways that seem out of character for them. It is still your responsibility, in my opinion, to strive to look for a positive interest even in the ugliest of circumstances.

Additionally, interests are not values. We hold a few core values close to our heart. Individuals and companies choose to live by those values. Core values might be integrity, honesty, or collaboration. If what you are asking someone to do would impact a core value, you will not reach an agreement. Values cannot be traded as interests can. You cannot ask a company that claims employee collaboration as a core value to treat its employees otherwise. It simply will not happen. Only once in more than five years have I stumbled upon a clash of values. I was mediating between neighbors who ultimately disagreed about raising children. That dispute was never resolved.

Use the lens that interests are always positive from the speaker's perspective to help you uncover hidden motivations.

If you truly want to be an effective negotiator, you have to be able to recognize your interests while also unearthing and addressing your counterpart's interests. Taking positions and reacting to your counterpart's positions will only lead to strained negotiation sessions and continuous misunderstandings. Use the tools laid out in this chapter to help you identify your interests, and identify those of your counterpart. You can then leverage shared interests into an agreement.

Chapter Three

..............................▶

Realistic Alternatives to a Negotiated Agreement

All negotiations have one global purpose: to continually determine if you are better off continuing to negotiate with your counterpart, or better off pursuing an alternative. This purpose encompasses meeting your goals or milestones while simultaneously weighing your alternatives should the negotiations fail to reach an agreement. There are two obvious aspects to this purpose. First, negotiators must come to the table ready to actively engage in the back and forth bargaining process. Second, negotiators should know what alternatives they have should the negotiations fail.

Unsuccessful negotiators fail to recognize or apply this purpose to their negotiations. Not only do they mistake simply meeting their goals for having a purpose, they cajole and coerce their counterpart. They use their time at the table to direct their attention to finding fault in their opponent's position, demanding that their opponent make concessions and defending their own position against attack. After the negotiations break down, and they often do break down under these circumstances, unsuccessful negotiators walk away from the table, often without any realistic plan for achieving their goals. These negotiators lack the tools to establish a back up plan. More importantly, even if they had a back up plan, they lack the tools to evaluate that plan against what is possible by continuing to negotiate. Consequently, they believe that walking away from the table will produce more desirable results than continuing to bargain.

In five years of mediating a variety of disputes, I have personally seen these two problems—substituting coercion for exploration and leaving to pursue untenable alternatives—surface in every setting I've been called into. When negotiators make these two mistakes their opponents perceive them as "difficult", which increases the tension at the table. Successful negotiators, however, rarely if ever fall into these two traps.

> **Your role at the bargaining table is to explore whether you can better satisfy your goals with a negotiated agreement than you could by singularly pursuing your alternatives.**

First of all, successful negotiators understand that their purpose is to explore all available options in an effort to narrow the list down to only those options that will effectively achieve their goals. This means that they are open to looking at things from their counterpart's perspective, to providing information about their own perspective and to creatively solving problems as they arise. Successful negotiators stay in conversations longer, and work harder to find common ground. Because successful negotiators have these traits they genuinely walk away from the table far less often than their unskilled counterparts. If they stay, you might ask, do they agree just to agree? My personal experience is that successful negotiators do not agree just to get it over with.

Successful negotiators have a keen awareness of all of the alternative paths to achieving their goals, and they don't deceive themselves about unrealistic alternatives. They factor in circumstances or costs that will impact the appeal of pursuing a particular alternative, such as opportunity costs or sunk costs. Furthermore, they use their creative problem solving skills to reach an agreement precisely because they realize that their alternatives may not help them reach their goals as effectively as an agreement would.

By reading this chapter you will have two helpful sets of tools. First, you will have the tools to bring an exploration framework to the conversation. This will prevent you from taking an overly aggressive or overly passive stance at the bargaining table. Second, you will have the tools to evaluate your alternatives to reaching a negotiated agreement. More importantly, you will have read some real life stories that demonstrate both unrealistic and realistic alternatives. These stories should help you better understand the efficacy of pursuing your alternatives should the negotiations break down.

Exploration

Your role at the bargaining table is to explore whether you can better satisfy your interests by negotiating an agreement than you could by singularly pursuing an alternative. Scholars coined the term **BATNA**, or **B**est **A**lternative to a **N**egotiated **A**greement to address this principle. The word *best* often obscures the point, which is identifying and evaluating all of your alternatives against the terms of a potential agreement. Negotiators somehow believe that a **BATNA** is synonymous with a silver bullet, often claiming that they have a **BATNA** without identifying realistic alternatives, let alone actually evaluating them against a negotiated agreement.

Looking at each interaction through the lens of exploration frees the negotiator to accept what is said and not said in a more neutral manner. Rather than feeling like he must defend his position or argue a point, successful negotiators use questions to mine for information about their counterparts perspective and assumptions, often finding that there is more common ground than initially apparent. In this place of exploration and neutrality, the skilled negotiator constantly weighs the likely outcome from a negotiated agreement against the likely outcome from an alternative path.

I want to be clear that I am not asking you to cave in to demands, or accept unreasonable behavior. I am asking that all negotiators have a more open mind. Rather than assuming that you know what your counterpart will or will not do, for example, be willing to explore by asking a series of questions. For a more visual image imagine that you are using sonar throughout the negotiation process. At every step of the process you are sending signals (asking questions) to find unseen obstacles and clear channels within which to navigate. You are also constantly testing the waters to determine if you would be better off pursuing some other alternative to meet your goals. Here are some generic questions that my clients have found useful. You might choose to ask yourself these questions, ask your counterpart, or develop some questions of your own.

- What is your company's greatest concern with . . . ?
- What bothers your company the most about that suggestion?
- What about . . . . is important to your company?
- Could you tell me more about . . . .
- What does . . . mean to your company?

By asking these or similar questions you are helping yourself determine if you will be able to meet your goals through an agreement with your counterpart. In addition to having an exploratory frame of mind, you also need to understand alternative paths to reaching your goals that do not include negotiating an agreement.

Alternatives to a Negotiated Agreement

Realistic best alternatives to a negotiated agreement are hard to come by. In order for an alternative to be considered a **BATNA**, it must get you substantially the same—if not better—result than a negotiated outcome would have gotten you. A **BATNA** is not any alternative to a negotiated outcome; it is the best alternative to a negotiated agreement. This is a difficult standard for an alternative to live up to; and, in fact, many alternatives fail miserably. What I find most fascinating is how intelligent people confuse unrealistic alternatives with their **BATNA.**

Unrealistic and Ineffective Alternatives

Unrealistic alternatives to a negotiated agreement have three common traits. First, they fail to get you the same or better result than if you had negotiated an agreement with your counterpart. Second, they require many moving parts to achieve your goals. Third, it takes too long to achieve a good result. Furthermore, unsuccessful negotiators aggregate several steps into one magical alternative, thereby, reaching an incomplete conclusion as to their alternatives. There are two common unrealistic alternatives that my client's have experienced: Litigation and customer's claims that they will move business to a competitor.

One example of an unrealistic alternative can be taking your counterpart to court. Litigation has a multitude of moving parts, from hiring the lawyer, to filing the suit, to navigating the legal procedures, to scheduling meetings, depositions and court

> **Successful negotiators have a keen awareness of all of the alternative paths to achieving their goals, and they don't deceive themselves about unrealistic alternatives.**

hearings. Any one of these moving parts can derail you and send you down the rabbit hole. Additionally, the litigation process is out of your control, while the negotiation process is firmly within your control. Lastly, you can lose a lot. Not just money, but time and peace of mind as the case winds it way through the labyrinthine legal system. Moreover, litigation is the aggregate of several alternatives, such as hiring an attorney and hiring an expert. You might reach a better result by taking any one step, say hiring an expert and returning to the bargaining table, than aggregating several steps and resolving to file a complaint in court. In addition to looking like the silver bullet that will meet one's goals, litigation feeds a common psychological trap most negotiators face at some point in their career.

Naive Realism

Litigants, as do many negotiators, suffer from a psychological tendency called Naïve Realism. Simply put for your purpose as a negotiator, your counterpart assumes, or even demands, that you see things as she sees them. Furthermore, their stated position assumes that everyone has the same set of facts and that everyone makes the same set of judgments about those facts. Perhaps the most obvious example is that between two warring departments competing for resources within the same company. One department eventually withdraws from the conversation and declares that someone higher in the organizational chart will have to make the decision. The withdrawing department implies that their superiors will agree with it and rule that the other department is unreasonable. The withdrawing department also thinks that the superiors will force the other department to moderate its unreasonable behavior. The assumption all along is that there is but one set of universal facts that must be interpreted in one universal way.

Unrealistic BATNA

The same circumstances that can make litigation unrealistic can also make using a new supplier unrealistic. This threat—that the customer will leave the bargaining table to start working with the vendor's competitor—is one that my clients hear the most often. In one instance, that threat turned out to be an unrealistic alternative to a negotiated agreement. The owner of a small, local manufacturing company told me that a Fortune 500 company demanded that her company lower its price. It claimed that it would not renew its contract with her company if she did not lower her price and instead move its business her competitor. The woman weighed all of her options and after some reflection chose not to lower her prices. She explained to me that while her competitor would agree to the artificially low price to win the business, she did not think that her competitor had the capital to immediately expand operations in order to accommodate the increased volume. She had a better handle on her customer's alternatives than they did. Only a few months later the Fortune 500 company re-initiated talks. Evidently, using the competitor was an unrealistic alternative in comparison to negotiating an agreement with her company in that the competitor did not offer the Fortune 500 company a substantially similar deal than the one they walked away from.

Furthermore, I suspect that the Fortune 500 company did not anticipate that the manufacturer would allow them to leave the table, which might have meant that they were not fully prepared to begin a new relationship with a new supplier. I've personally found that large companies have not vetted the alternative supplier, choosing instead to use the alternative supplier's name as a stick only to get my client (their preferred supplier) to lower the price. If these examples are not realistic alternatives, what could be considered a realistic alternative, let alone a **B**est **A**lternative to a **N**egotiated **A**greement?

Realistic and Effective Alternatives

A **BATNA** is a path to meeting your needs in a substantially similar or better way than what an agreement would have provided. A **BATNA** might be using your sales resources to secure a different marquee customer, or effectively invoking the provisions of a contract. For these two examples to be considered realistic or better than negotiating an agreement, the negotiator would have to be satisfied that pursuing the alternative was not only realistic but that at the end of the transaction the negotiator's company was in as good of a position, if not better, than had his company stuck it out with their counterpart. As it turns out, these two examples were **BATNA's**.

Securing a Different Anchor Customer. A good example of a realistic **BATNA** occurred a couple of years ago. A manufacturing company was planning to open a new plant in a midwestern city. Part of my client's strategy was to secure a particular new customer, who would agree to order a minimum volume of business. After several meetings between the manufacturer and the potential customer, the negotiations were called off. The manufacturer had a realistic alternative in place. It changed course and secured a larger contract with an existing customer, which included moving that customer's business to the new plant. The plant was now financially viable without the potential customer's business. The manufacturer then returned to the potential customer, resumed negotiations and secured a contract on completely different terms. There were no promises of meeting minimum volumes in the new agreement. The manufacturer's **BATNA** allowed it to secure enough business to justify opening the plant without depending on the potential customer's commitment to purchase a minimum volume of goods. In this new agreement both the manufacturer and the customer got what they wanted—a plant with enough income to justify its existence without the contractual promise of a minimum volume of goods.

The difference between this example, characterized as realistic, and the one above, characterized as unrealistic, is that in my client's case, they were pursuing a viable back up plan with an existing customer while they were negotiating with the potential customer. They weren't bluffing when they left the table. Furthermore, my client continually evaluated their alternatives against what was possible with the potential customer. This allowed them to see that they could meet the potential customer's demands without jeopardizing their bottom line. After walking away from the deal as proposed by the potential customer, they were able to return to the potential customer with an altered agreement that met customer's desire not to commit to minimum volumes after they meet their own financial needs. Above all, the manufacturer's executives retained an air of exploration that allowed them to be truly creative.

Invoking the Provisions of the Contract. A colleague explained a recent negotiation to me in which his client had a marvelous **BATNA** written right into the terms of an agreement. The circumstances involved a shareholders agreement, vested shares in a privately held company and company directors who were completely unwilling to negotiate. Valuing small, privately held companies is not an exact science and the company's directors thought that they could force a shareholder to accept a ridiculously low offer. Furthermore, this company had no alternatives to negotiating with the shareholder, although no one on their side considered that when they asked the shareholder to give back his shares.

The shareholder had a **BATNA** written into the fine print. In the shareholder's agreement the method for buying back the shares and the price for the buy back were outlined. All the shareholder had to do was follow the agreement to the letter to resolve the dispute. Because of the company's intransigence, the company forced the shareholder from the table and a mutually agreed price per share to the strictures of the agreement, which had a high, pre-determined price per share. The shareholder had the realistic alternative to a negotiated agreement. He simply had to invoke the terms of the shareholder's agreement. The point of this story to reinforce in you as a negotiator two things: Most negotiators don't really have an alternative to negotiating with you and the answer you are looking for just might be spelled out for you in the fine print.

Four Helpful Questions

As these stories point out, evaluating your alternatives against the possibilities of negotiating an agreement is a critical, and overlooked, part of the negotiation process. Evaluating alternatives should be done before any counteroffers are made or any actions taken that could force a party from the table. Use the following questions as a tool to help you evaluate the efficacy of your alternatives.

- What can you do all by yourself to pursue your goals?
- Looking at your underlying motivations for wanting this agreement, might there be another way to achieve your goals?
- Which alternatives would get you substantially the same if not a better result than negotiating an agreement with your counterpart?
- If you are reluctant to pursue your alternatives, can you bring in a third party or third party information to further your goals? (Are there opinions from recognized industry experts or agreed upon industry performance standards that could move talks along?)

When working as the mediator, I would invite both parties to explore all of her options. By asking them to answer these questions for me, they were better able to determine for themselves what were realistic and unrealistic alternatives if they were unable to reach an agreement. I did not have to evaluate for them the costs of pursuing their alternatives against the process of reaching an agreement with their counterpart.

A BATNA is a path to meeting your needs in a substantially similar or better way than what an agreement would have provided.

Not thinking through your alternatives to negotiating an agreement leaves you in one of two places. First you may give in out of fear that you have no alternatives, when you might have perfectly good alternatives. Second, you might walk away from a deal that is better than your alternative will provide. Evaluating your alternatives requires consideration of alternatives that you control, the consequences of your actions and also recognizing hidden costs and benefits associated with the alternative. Moreover, you have to honestly appraise the total deal value—not come to a knee jerk reaction like *that's not enough*. As you develop the skills to evaluate and measure your alternatives against a negotiated deal, you will find that some of the deals you would have accepted you now reject, and the deals you might have rejected you now accept. It is all because you now have a much clearer picture of your alternatives.

Chapter Four

.......................➤

Effectively Negotiating Price

There are some predicable negotiation patterns when money is an issue. Understanding these patterns will give you a tremendous advantage at the bargaining table. Successful negotiators trust and understand the flow of negotiating money. They instinctively understand and respect that a back and forth process is necessary to arrive at a final number. Unsuccessful negotiators, on the other hand, derisively call it horse trading and often resent the process.

To further complicate matters, haggling over money is fraught with fears; fear that I'll leave money on the table, fear that I'll get taken to the cleaners, fear that I'll look like a fool if I don't drive a hard bargain. These fears dominate the bargaining process causing some negative consequences. Negotiators often act against their true motivations, such as establishing a long term partnership with a supplier, by focusing solely on price to the detriment

There are some predictable negotiation patterns when money is an issue. Understanding those patterns will give you a tremendous advantage at the bargaining table.

of other tangible and intangible factors. Furthermore, some negotiators unwittingly set their counterpart up to react in increasingly combative ways by making unusually high or low offers on the price of goods or services. In fact, this style is justified by those teaching negotiation skills to professional purchasers as the way it has to be done adding that the push/pull of these conversations provides cost savings. This is the ugly, competitive aspect of negotiations that least represents the spirit of win/win negotiations.

This competitive, combative atmosphere is a real turn off for most ordinary negotiators. They learn to distrust, rather than appreciate, the back and forth process. They think that if everyone just played fair everyone could get to a good price right off the bat. I've watched these well meaning negotiators short cut bargaining process and make opening offers that left them no room within which to bargain. A colleague told a room filled with more than 150 mediators a story that illustrates this point.

My colleague is a professional mediator. During his divorce, he and his soon to be ex-wife attended a settlement conference. As he tells the story, he thought that they were both "adults" so the back and forth bargaining process was not necessary. My colleague threw out a settlement number that he thought was fair, representing the middle between two extreme settlement numbers. His ex's attorney countered with a much higher settlement offer. To my colleague's surprise, he — a highly skilled negotiator — was negotiating at much higher settlement range than he anticipated! He made a mistake that every negotiator makes at some point in time. He underestimated the desire we humans have to haggle over money.

Haggling over price is actually a very valuable part of the entire negotiation process. Haggling allows us to evaluate our opponent, establish the value of our goods and services, and most importantly, it gives us a chance to make tradeoffs.

It is through this give and take that we become satisfied that we got a fair deal. Some of you might be thinking, *My customers don't want to haggle. They want the lowest price upfront or we're out the door.*

Most people when spending their own money want value for their dollar. The problem in business to business negotiations is that no one is spending their own money. To make matters worse, some companies reward their buyers on cost savings, which leads to frustrating conversations that have nothing to do with the value of the product or service. The end user of your product or service, though, is very interested in value. By understanding the predictability of negotiating money, you can better manage price only conversations with purchasers and the value conversation with end users.

Haggling allows us to evaluate our opponent, establish the value of our goods and services, and most importantly, it gives us a chance to make tradeoffs. It is through this give and take that we become satisfied that we got a fair deal.

The tools that I discuss in this chapter are based upon research done by many negotiation scholars. Distributive bargaining is a term for explaining the behavior when humans haggle over money. While this and other terms are not generally used in day-to-day conversations, the actual processes described are used everyday by ordinary, business people.

This chapter will offer you three very important keys to unlock the mystery of predicting money negotiations. First, you will have a clear, down to earth understanding of the patterns of negotiating money. No longer will you lack the vocabulary to express what is happening at the bargaining table. Second, you will have a better understanding of one significant psychological tendency that impacts money negotiations. By recognizing this tendency, you can use it to your advantage or avoid having it used against you. Finally, you will have a tangible method for predicting the flow of money before you ever start a conversation with your counterpart.

Plotting Money Negotiations

My experience taught me that most people instinctively understand what is happening when money is being negotiated, but don't have the vocabulary to describe their experience. Like other successful negotiators, I too instinctively knew what would happen when I would negotiate numbers with opposing counsel, but it wasn't until 2003 that I discovered that what I intuitively anticipated could be mapped out in a logical manner. After successfully using tools that I developed for myself, I began teaching other mediators about the predictability of negotiating money. Using my tools, they too were able to understand and predict what could happen when negotiating money. The diagrams that follow are meant to visually illustrate a "horse trade." I combine these diagrams with terms to further convey the process.

Imagine that the diagrams that follow[1] represent an American football goal post, and as a negotiator you must kick your ball (the final number for a product or service) between the two vertical bars in order to get your point—the deal. (If you are not an American football fan, allow me the use of this analogy.) In football, a team can score a point(s) if the football travels between the two upright bars. Using this same analogy, negotiators also try to get their deal to travel between two vertical bars. These bars are the walk away points in the deal.

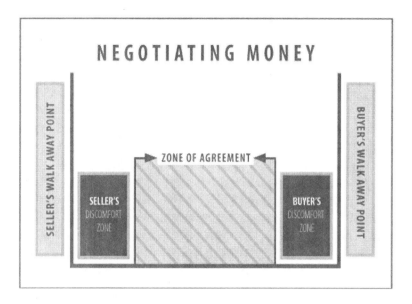

Walk Away Points

A walk away point represents the number at which one negotiator will determine it is better to walk away from the bargaining table than to make a counteroffer. The number thrown out is either so high or so low, that the negotiator knows that she cannot not spend any more of her time trying to haggle with her counterpart. This walk away point is a tangible number and must be distinguished from walking away used as a tactic to force the other side into a concession. For this discussion, a walk away point is actually the point at which it fails to make financial sense to continue to talk to the other side.

As I mentioned, many negotiators instinctively react to "highball" or "lowball" offers. Negotiators may be surprised, offended or even angry at the insult of such an offer. Several of my clients expressed these reactions to ridiculous offers. To refer back to the diagram, my client's reaction reflected that the highball or lowball offer traveled outside of the vertical bars. Again, I am speaking of a genuine reaction, not a negotiating ploy. An example will help make this concept clearer.

Let's say that you manufacture widgets. You know that the total cost to manufacture the widget is $1.[2] That includes all the costs of goods sold, including overhead, labor and materials. Any buyer who offers you 99 cents for the widget is in your walk away zone. You cannot, and should not, sell your product for 99 cents. Even if you sell one million widgets, you are losing money and at your walk away point, because you are losing one penny per widget at the end of the day.

At the other end, let's say that while you manufacture the widget for $1, your counterpart can only afford to pay $10 for the widget. If you offer the widget for sale at $11, you will technically be in the buyer's walk away point. No matter how lovely your widget, the buyer cannot afford to pay more than $10 for it. I mean really afford only $10, not just what they would like to pay for it, which would be substantially less so they could also make a profit.

> **A walk away point is actually the point at which it fails to make financial sense to continue to talk to the other side.**

Estimating the Other Party's Walk Away Point

The question you may be asking yourself right now is *How do I know my counterpart's walk away point?* In short, you will never know exactly where that point is. All you will ever know for sure is what you can control. Since you cannot control your counterpart, or know your counterpart's finances, you will never know for sure your counterpart's true walk away number. That fact leaves most negotiators with the impression that they should let the other guy make the first offer. Many feel that if they make the first offer they will undershoot or overshoot the price, so they allow their counter part to establish the price. The old wives tale that one should always allow the other person to throw out the first number is actually wrong in many circumstances and will be discussed at greater length below.

Use the previous diagram to plot out walk away numbers. You should always know your number and have somewhat of an idea of your counterpart's number. The more you discipline yourself to analyze your negotiations in this manner, the better feel you will have for your counterpart's walk away number.

Discomfort Zone

Immediately within the vertical bars are the discomfort zones. I coined the term discomfort zone when I realized that when negotiators talked about their bottom line at the bargaining table, what they were really talking about was the point at which they were uncomfortable with the price. When negotiators find themselves within in their discomfort zone, some interesting behaviors assert themselves. People become defensive or aggressive and can easily revert to very positional bargaining using language to indicate that they are not really willing to engage in the back and forth process with their counterpart.

Looking at the diagram on page 33, just to the right of the left vertical line is the sellers discomfort zone. This is a price at which the seller will agree, but feels some discomfort. For what ever reason, the seller believes that the price is too low. My experience as a mediator suggests that business disagreements begin as agreements to numbers that land in a discomfort zone. Once one party feels taken advantage of, they will look for ways to right that wrong. Maybe they add other charges. Maybe they cut back on service. In any event, the final price landed in the discomfort zone and they now will take action to make up the perceived difference between that final price and what they think they deserve.

Looking at the diagram on page 33, just to the left of the right vertical line is the buyers discomfort zone. Similar to the seller in the example above, buyers who land in their discomfort zone will jettison the agreement at the first hint that they can find a better price elsewhere.

But I Must Agree to Their Number. At this point, I will digress to talk about what I suspect many of you are thinking. *In this competitive market I have no choice but to agree to a number in my discomfort zone. If I don't, the business will go elsewhere.* "While this might be a valid argument, agreeing to a number that places you at a financial disadvantage is unwise for your company and, believe it or not unwise for your counterpart too.

I was a catalyst for a verbal altercation between a small company owner and a professional buyer from a Fortune 500. Several years ago, I was speaking to a group of businesses that supply products and services to prime contractors to the US Department of Energy. Suddenly, a small company owner began yelling at a buyer from a prime contractor, "You people are trying to put me out of business!" While my trial experience prepared me for all types of unexpected events, I had not seen this one coming. The buyer said the most interesting thing in response. "It is not my job to make sure that you make a profit. That is your job. Now, if you fail I fail and that would

Agreeing to a number that places you at a financial disadvantage is unwise for your company and, believe it or not for your counterpart too.

make me look bad. I don't want you to fail, but don't look to me to look out for you." Not only had the buyer handled the situation well, I agreed with him whole heartedly and said so publicly.

It is not the other company's responsibility to protect your company's profitability. You must protect your company financially, and you must also not make any one else look bad for making an unwise choice in working with your company. That means you must negotiate and advocate for your company even in the face of pressure to concede to a very low price. Other chapters in the book will help outline strategies, tactics and processes for making counteroffers, all of which will help manage high stakes, high pressure negotiations.

Before agreeing to a number in your discomfort zone, do the requisite research. In my experience working with companies, many

- underestimate their costs, or have an inaccurate financial picture,
- feel pressured to accept the buyer's arbitrary number,
- accept unfounded assertions about competitors in the market place,
- fail to anticipate hidden agendas, and
- generally do not have any idea about their opponents alternatives to negotiating.

It is in the haze that businesses find themselves agreeing to numbers that they later regret. The flip side, in my experience, is that buyers, particularly at very large corporations,

- fail to understand how the widget or service improves the corporation's bottom line,
- see the widget or service as a "purchase" and subject to a line item in the budget,
- compare apples to tomatoes claiming it's all fruit , and

- over estimate the effectiveness of pursuing other alternatives or vendors.

These misconceptions lead to deals that look good on paper, but are actually so one sided as to lead to feelings of distrust or even disloyalty throughout the remainder of the relationship. Deals that land more closely within the middle of the diagram are more sustainable for all parties.

Zone of Agreement

In the middle of the diagram on page 33 lies the Zone of Agreement. This zone of agreement is the place at which parties are statistically likely to reach an agreement. Using the same numbers from the example above, technically all the prices between $1 (seller's walk away point) and $10 (buyer's walk away point) are considered within the zone of agreement. Those negotiations that result in agreements on price that are more likely to hover around the $5 mark are equally satisfying and unsatisfying. Meaning, both the seller and the buyer are happy not to be in their discomfort zone, but they think that they could have gotten a better deal. From my point of view, deals that land closer to the middle are more accurately labeled in the zone of agreement.

At any negotiation session, one party has to start the conversation. Unsuccessful negotiators often believe that they have more to gain my allowing their counterpart to throw out the first number. Those who do often succumb to one particularly strong psychological tendency called a negotiation anchor.

Negotiation Anchors

A negotiation anchor is much like a boat anchor. Once the captain lowers the anchor, the boat will circle the anchor within a radius created by the length of chain connecting the anchor to the boat. Unless the anchor is disconnected or lifted, the boat will not stray. In negotiations, the first number thrown out is an anchor. Like a boat anchor, that number settles the parties into a smaller zone of agreement than had been apparent. And, like a boat anchor, it can prevent parties from reaching beyond the area created by the anchor.

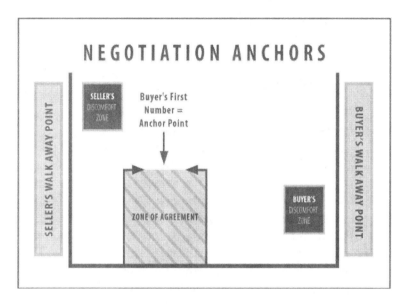

As the chart above demonstrates, the party that tosses out the first number actually has quite a bit of power to anchor the negotiations at a point at which it feels comfortable, or which it believes gives it the greatest advantage. Therefore, making an opening offer is actually a very powerful step to take in the negotiation process.

Unsuccessful negotiators usually have one reaction to negotiation anchors. They will start calculating counteroffers based on that anchor, ignoring the range of possibilities that existed before the anchor was established. Using the same scenario above, if the buyer throws out a price of $3 for your widget, most negotiators will use $3 as a starting point to

A negotiation anchor is much like a boat anchor. Once the captain lowers the anchor, the boat will circle the anchor within a radius created by the length of chain connecting the anchor to the boat.

calculate a counteroffer. The end result is a zone of agreement that has narrowed significantly. Negotiating $3 or $4 for the widget seems realistic until you realize that all the numbers from $4 to $9.99 (including the buyers discomfort zone) were at play.

Recognizing that an opening offer has an anchoring effect, successful negotiators will calculate a whole range of counteroffers, including offers that stretch the zone of agreement beyond the range established by the anchor. Doing this requires planning because successful negotiators understand that a counteroffer outside of the newly created zone of agreement may make the other party uncomfortable. That reason alone is not reason enough though not to make a more aggressive counteroffer than you had intended.

Stretching Beyond the Anchor

A large company approached my client, a technology start-up, with an acquisition plan. The large company was a long time customer with many years of experience working with my client. When they approached the start-up with the proposal, they asked my client to name their purchase price. Remembering the impact negotiation anchors have on the process, my client declined. My client did not know enough about valuing itself as a strategic acquisition to make that opening offer. The acquiring company made an initial offer and by doing so set the anchor. The following diagrams represent the flow of the negotiations from this point forward.

This diagram shows the buyers initial purchase price for the seller's company, and the newly created zone of agreement. It also represents the seller's counteroffer.

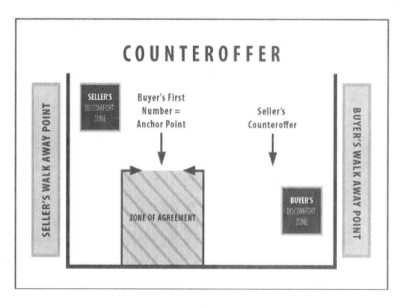

As you can see, the counteroffer pushed beyond the limits of the zone of agreement and landed (as we later learned) near their discomfort zone.

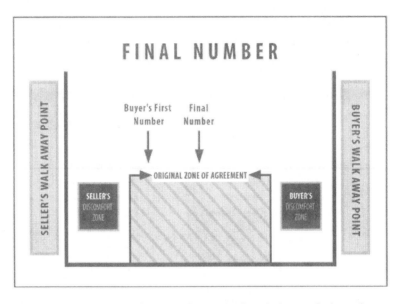

This diagram shows the final purchase price in relation to the buyer's initial offer. The final price landed within the original zone of agreement. As a result, my clients netted much more than had they used the buyer's initial offer to calculate their counteroffer.

My client had three goals after it received the opening offer. First, it wanted to use one common language to establish value, not just price. Second, it wanted to reach an agreement on value, and price, that was in the middle of the two walk away points, as opposed to the zone of agreement created by the anchor point. Three, it wanted to use the negotiation process to enhance the business relationship between the two companies. My client was also aware that their counterpart was not expecting an aggressive counteroffer. Anticipating push back, my client used its knowledge of money negotiations to carefully plan the conversations in order to achieve all three aims.

This back and forth process about price included

conversations about value, resulting in fruitful dialogue about how my client's company would significantly increase profitability. In the end, the final purchase price landed between the two walk away points. Each negotiator felt equally satisfied thinking they got their counterpart to move off of his original position.

As this example illustrates, there are clear patterns when negotiating money. Accepting and understanding these patters will give you an advantage at the bargaining table. Furthermore, you now have the vocabulary to express what is happening at the bargaining table. You and your colleagues can distinguish a true walk away point from a negotiation tactic aimed at getting you to concede. Finally, you have a tangible method for predicting the flow of money before you ever start a conversation with your counterpart.

It is goes without saying that most negotiations can be mapped out using my diagram. While there might be circumstances in which these charts do not apply, I urge you to still look at your negotiations through this distributive lens. It will assure you a process to plot out some numbers that you do know, plot out some numbers that are educated guesses, and allow you to see clearly what you do not know enough about before making or allowing the other party to make an offer.

Chapter Five

························▶

Making Effective Tradeoffs

Negotiators focus attention on making tradeoffs in order to satisfy the other party's needs while simultaneously satisfying their own. Tradeoffs are a significant method for tailoring deals to meet both companies' needs. Properly defined, a tradeoff is something that you offer the other party in exchange for something of value in return. The tradeoff can be either tangible or intangible, and in many circumstances you have indentified items in advance to use tradeoffs. Any single item is then offered to your counterpart in exchange for something from his company that has value to your company. This is important. In order for something to be really considered a tradeoff, you must get something of value in return. Concessions, on the other hand, are things that you give without any expectation that you will receive anything in return.

Successful negotiators carefully choose when to make tradeoffs and when to make concessions. They understand that each sets a particular tone and establishes a precedent. Concessions have a take it or leave it tone, while tradeoffs invite both

Are you giving too much away? Start making tradeoffs, not concessions.

negotiators to continue the conversation. Concessions are often taken for granted, meaning many customers assume that a sales professional will want to give them something for the privilege of winning their company's business. I often hear statements like, "we need such-and-such price, so if you want our business you will have to lower your price." Implicit in this statement is the understanding that the customer will get all the bells and whistles and will not be asked to reciprocate. They are expecting you to concede, lower the price and not request any modification to the deal on their part. Tradeoffs, on the other hand, are explicit intentions to barter one thing for another. Tradeoffs are not taken for granted and many negotiators will have several conversations before finding the right mix of items to trade back and forth.

My pet peeve with the negotiation literature is that all too often authors refer to concessions and tradeoffs interchangeably, meaning they talk about tradeoffs but call them concessions or worse, call concessions tradeoffs. Mixing these terms creates confusion in the literature and during the actual back and forth bartering. Unsuccessful negotiators don't distinguish between offering something without an expectation of getting something in return, and offering something with the explicit understanding that the only way their counterpart will benefit is to offer something in return. I see many negotiators make concessions believing that they are making tradeoffs just to become disappointed or upset that they did not get anything in return.

The problem is that unsuccessful negotiators think that by making a concession the other party will naturally make a concession in return. Because of the highly competitive nature of some negotiations, an unspoken rule may actually prevent such reciprocity. I've heard negotiators say, "if they don't ask, I don't offer." Without any explicit obligation of reciprocity, the negotiator has just made a concession, not a tradeoff.

Furthermore, some companies do not always think in terms of tradeoffs when working with their suppliers. In fact, some professional buyers speak primarily in terms of concessions. From their point of view, there are some good reasons. Enterprise companies do not have the bandwidth to create a fully tailored agreement with every vendor. By the very nature of their size, they need uniformity. Additionally, the people creating these agreements might not be the ultimate decision maker, limiting their ability to make tradeoffs. More importantly, the person you work with might be so far removed from the end goal of how your product or service will be used that tradeoffs may seem less meaningful to them.

To make effective tradeoffs, you must know what your counterpart is willing to accept from you, and what you are willing to accept from him in exchange.

I taught a negotiation skills class at a MBA program and had the privilege to get to know a buyer from a Fortune 500 company. Our conversations opened my eyes to the limitations on his bargaining power. I also learned that buyers are always on the lookout for price concessions. If you are able to explain a tradeoff and sell the value of the tradeoff, the buyer might be willing to run it up the chain of command. The lesson I learned is that it is your responsibility to respond to requests for concessions with a request for a tradeoff, even when negotiating with a very large company.

This chapter will address two important factors in making effective tradeoffs. First, you will have a clearer understanding of the role reciprocity takes at the bargaining table. By understanding the limitations of this psychological tendency, you will better understand why some conversations lead to concessions, while others lead to a fair exchange of tradeoffs. Second, you will learn four best practices for making effective tradeoffs. Having these tools at your disposal will make you a much more effective negotiator.

The Obligation of Reciprocity

The Obligation of Reciprocity is a fairly straight forward psychological principle. It works like this: If you do something nice for me, I will feel obligated to do something nice for you in return. We teach our children this lesson from the time they are two years old. We learn to share and help one another out. Unsuccessful negotiators assume that since they work from this principle this common sense principle will come into play at the bargaining table too. I find there are three reasons that negotiators don't immediately respond to this principle.

First, some negotiators do not think that it is their job to offer you anything just because you offered them something. I've read articles written for professional buyers working within large corporations who suggest that buyers are not under any obligation to offer suppliers anything when they ask the supplier to make a price concession. Truth be told, I also happen to fall into that category of negotiators. Now that I am aware that I have this instinct, I make conscious choices to override it in some circumstances by offering to make an unsolicited tradeoff. I must admit though that it is not natural for me to offer something without being explicitly asked. And, I am not alone.

A fellow mediator told me a story some years back about a family mediation that she participated in. Two divorced parents came to a community mediation center to resolve conflicts about visitation with their children. In a confidential and private meeting between Dad and the mediator, Dad agreed to make some accommodations if Mom agreed to make some modifications to the visitation schedule. The mediator brought Mom and Dad together to talk about the tradeoffs that they each had agreed to make in their confidential meetings with the mediator. Mom started the session by agreeing to make the schedule changes, while Dad sat quietly. Not once did Dad offer to make the accommodations that he told the mediator he would be willing to make. Because of confidentiality rules, the mediator was barred from making any mention of Dad's conversation with her to Mom. Mom and Dad signed a new visitation schedule and left the center. Before Dad got on the elevator the mediator asked him privately why he hadn't offered to make the accommodations. He said, "she never asked me to." I'll grant you that there were a lot of personal, family dynamics also at play, but I submit that his attitude is not uncommon. In fact, I believe it is your responsibility to ask for tradeoffs during a bargaining session. The next two paragraphs explain why.

The second reason negotiators don't make tradeoffs is that the receiving party does not know how to reciprocate. My experience has taught me that this is by far is the most prevalent reason unsuccessful negotiators don't offer their counterpart anything in return for a unilateral concession made by their counterpart. It is your responsibility to make clear requests otherwise your counterpart will not know what to offer you when the time arrives to reciprocate.

The third reason is the flip side of the second reason. You, as the offering party, do not know what you want from your counterpart. It makes it so hard for your counterpart to reciprocate if you yourself don't even know what it is that you are willing to accept. It is not that uncommon for unsuccessful negotiators to not know what they are willing to accept as a tradeoff from their counterpart.

At all of my training sessions, I pair people up and ask one partner to get their partner to agree to do something, such as to cross the room. Training participants offer their partners a dollar, lunch, or the gigantic blueberry muffin that they got on the way in. Rarely do these bribes work. Their partner stands there saying things like, "one dollar is not enough" or "I brought my lunch" or "I don't like blueberries." The lessons are always the same. To make effective tradeoffs, you must know what your counterpart is willing to accept from you, and what you are willing to accept from her in exchange.

Concessions are items that you give up at the bargaining table while expecting to receive nothing in return.

Now that you understand why people are less likely to spontaneously reciprocate, let's talk about what you can do to maximize the likelihood that the other party will acknowledge your tradeoffs and respond in kind. There are four strategies that I suggest you use when making tradeoffs.

Maximizing Tradeoffs[1]

First, you need to label any conversation in which you intend to offer something to your counterpart as a tradeoff. Let the other negotiator know that you are making a tradeoff by using the word tradeoff somewhere in your sentence. I suggest, "what if we were to make the following tradeoff . . .?" Don't assume that the other person will understand the importance of what you are offering, or respond in kind without giving them a verbal cue.

Second, you must be very precise in your request by defining the scope of the tradeoff. Meaning, not only must you be clear in what you are offering, you must also clear about what you are expecting in return. A couple of years ago, I was negotiating face-to-face with the bigwig from a large company and very clearly offered a tradeoff, which he initially chose to ignore. Our negotiation team continued to stress that we were offering a tradeoff and not a concession. Being clear that we were offering only a tradeoff helped us maintain the profitability of the contract. Defining the scope of the tradeoff will not always mean an equal exchange, but it will give you greater success than not defining one at all.

Third, use contingent language. I suggest "if-then" statements to convey the contingent nature of the tradeoff. In my example above, I put the tradeoff in the "if-then" framework. For example, I said something like, "If you are willing to remove the chargeback provisions, we would be willing to offer your company another 2% discount." This framework is significant because by linking tradeoffs together, you can withdraw your portion of the tradeoff if the other negotiator cannot, or will not, offer you what you want in return. This offers you some protection from being taken advantage of.

Finally, make tradeoffs in installments. I know that this seems obvious enough, but my husband tells a very funny story about a college housemate many years ago who was selling something door-to-door. (It was long before the internet.) The housemate came back within an hour or two having sold all of his wares. When my husband asked how he did it, the housemate said, "I gave the customers the whole deal all at once. I didn't waste time offering this, then that and so on." While this freed the housemate up to goof off, it cost the company a great deal in lost profit margin. It is this sense of horse trading, or making tradeoffs in installments that is at the heart of real bargaining; it is also the thing some people like the least. Keep in mind that making installments in increments not only preserves your bottom line, it also garners respect from the other side. Negotiators who give it all away may be seen as lazy, and will set up the expectation that they will always give it all away.

Tradeoffs are at the heart of the back and forth nature of negotiation. Tradeoffs can help both parties create an agreement that better meets their needs, while also maintaining your company's bottom line. Concessions, while also a part of the bargaining process, should be offered cautiously and after careful consideration as to your company's bottom line and its continuing relationship with your counterpart. Concessions should be treated as a unilateral gift to the other party. Your counterpart might respond in kind, or they might not. If you keep in mind that tradeoffs force the obligation of reciprocity, while a concession only invites it, you will be far more clear about what you are willing to give away asking for what you want in return.

Chapter Six

.....................................▶

Making Effective Counteroffers

Effective counteroffers are properly structured and well timed. A counteroffer is a change that you make to your counterpart's existing proposal. Making a unilateral change to your own proposal it is not a counteroffer; you are negotiating against yourself. An effective counteroffer is one that the other party accepts outright, or makes only minor changes before accepting it because they recognize that it meets their needs. An ineffective counteroffer is one that is rejected outright, is all about what you cannot do for the other party and is poorly timed, usually coming too soon in the back and forth exchange of information. Because successful negotiators understand the process of making counteroffers, they are more likely to take the time to structure their counteroffers.

I use the word structure very deliberately. My experience as a mediator and negotiation coach taught me that many unsuccessful negotiators had not prepared any counteroffer before entering a negotiation, and when they did try to make a counterproposal it was shot down. The mediation clients would ask me, "What

Making a unilateral change to your own proposal it is not a counteroffer; you are negotiating against yourself.

happened? I was sure that the solution I offered solved the problem." Their solution might have solved the problem, but the content, delivery and timing were all wrong. It is not that unsuccessful negotiators don't have the right answer; it's that they give the right answer all wrong.

Unsuccessful negotiators make two common mistakes when they attempt to make counterproposals: They either throw out a solution too early in the process, before their counter part has explained what is important to her, or they fail to consider whether their proposal meets their counterpart's needs from *their counterpart's perspective*.

Perspective is the key. Good solutions get shot down because the receiver has not made the connection that the counterproposal will meet her needs. Often, the receiver has in her mind a specific, detailed solution and this solution is their offer to you. Any change to their offer — even if it makes things better — is not always recognized as a better solution. For this reason alone, many perfectly good counteroffers are rejected. It is your job as a skilled negotiator to present the counterproposal in such as way as to signal to your counterpart that your offer meets their needs. Furthermore, your counterpart at this point in the process does not care one wit about what you can or cannot do. They might care later, but not when you are making changes to their offer or proposal.

Successful negotiators, on the other hand, understand that the counterproposal should explicitly communicate two things: 1) That you are meeting your counterparts needs, and 2) that you are open to engage in a back and forth conversation until the solution meets everyone's needs. Because the back and forth process scares and intimidates some people, successful negotiators take the time to structure the offer and the atmosphere in order to purposely create a cordial back and forth process.

One of my clients, a technology company, made a successful, albeit financially aggressive, counterproposal. In working with me, they took the time to think about things that many ordinary negotiators fail to consider such as establishing the factual information supporting their counterproposal in a way that was well received. They also considered the format of the conversation and the timing of both the information exchange and the delivery of the actual number. They netted millions more from the deal by being thoughtful about crafting their strategic counteroffer than had they jumped in with a counteroffer right after their counterpart made their offer. Effectively making counterproposals is not only financially beneficial, it is also a great way to establish a good working relationship with your counterpart.

You can stay genuinely curious during any negotiation by disciplining yourself to ask clarifying questions.

After reading this chapter, you will know how to properly structure, time and deliver your counterproposals. There are four elements that you need to consider before making a counteroffer. The first element is using a communication technique that allows you to test assumptions about tradeoffs before you actually make them. The second element is what I call sequencing, meaning putting the information that you gather from the communication technique in the right order for maximum receptivity. The third element is timing the counteroffer. There are two obvious timing methods that I will discuss. Finally, the last element is the delivery of the message. In an increasingly electronic world, you should not expect that you can meet face to face to "hash things out."

Clarifying Questions

All good negotiators communicate their interests, whether in their offers or in the tradeoffs they make. Highly successful negotiators, on the other hand, know how to get their counterpart to communicate their interests and then use that information to make effective counteroffers. Communicating at the bargaining table is one part listening for what is not being said as well as one part listening for what is being said.

I learned the importance of listening for both types of information as a mediator. As an independent observer, I learned to listen more carefully to what a party was not saying as that also had an impact on the resolution of the issue. Fascinated by the realization that people communicate by not saying certain things, I began to ask questions that tested my assumptions. I thought to myself, *Were they really not communicating clearly or were they playing hide the ball?*

Clarifying questions allow the speaker to talk at length about a topic that is important to them. These questions are expansive, open ended questions that mine for information in a gentle way. To my surprise, almost everyone responds well to clarifying questions. Part of their allure is that the questions themselves do not harbor a hidden agenda. The receiver can take the question at face value without worrying about being tricked. The other part of the allure of these questions is that the receiver gets to talk about what they want to talk about. Today, people are so rushed and disconnected from one another that they rarely experience the pleasure of being able to talk about what matters to them.

As a skilled negotiator, you play two roles: Genuinely curious questioner and tight-lipped listener. In order for these questions to work their magic, you must be genuinely curious about what the answer will be. If you are condescending or sarcastic, you will definitely get a controlled, defensive response, which will often fail to give you the information you need. Once you've asked the question, you need to shut up. I mean it. You don't say a word until you are sure that the person has completed their thought. Clarifying questions often evoke a paragraph response, so you need to be prepared to listen for several sentences suppressing your urge to interrupt. Here are my favorite nine clarifying questions, and one clarifying statement:

- What is your greatest concern with . . . ?
- What bothers you the most about that suggestion?
- What about . . . . is important to you?
- Tell me more about . . . . .
- What does . . . look like to you?
- How can we make our proposal fit your need to {spell their need and/or interest out}?
- What is the most/least important thing you need from us?
- How important is . . . to the overall picture?
- How do you see that we can accomplish . . .?
- If you were in my shoes, what would you recommend?

Not rocket science I know. They are deceptively simple and incredibly effective at getting past the hidden agenda's that can derail the best intentioned counteroffer. Your challenge is to resist the urge to have all the answers and ask one of these questions instead.

I get the most push back from the last question. It can be scary for most negotiators to risk looking like they are giving up control by asking someone for their advice. If used at the right time, though, this question can reveal a lot about your counterpart's intentions–good and bad.

A non-profit client of mine successfully used this question, "If you were in my shoes, what would you recommend?" to break down the wall that was preventing it from reaching an agreement with their counterpart. The non-profit and a state agency had been negotiating over the course of several years when the non-profit finally walked away from the table. Because of pressure from many sources, the non-profit felt compelled to make one more attempt to negotiate a favorable agreement. After I worked with the board and the executive director, we all decided that the non-profit had nothing to lose from asking one question. Completely exasperated, the executive director sat down with a state employee and asked her, "If you were in my shoes, what would you do?" To the director's surprise, the state employee laid out a plan of action that we had never considered. She also revealed in very subtle ways the internal blocks that were preventing her from agreeing to our terms. In the end, not more than thirty days after that pivotal conversation, the non-profit and the head of the state agency reached an agreement in principle on many key issues. This agreement was signed and presented to the chairman of the board at the annual fund raising dinner. Many months later all of the individual agreements were drafted, signed and put into place.

Sometimes the other party wants to tell you something but cannot come right out and say it. If you offer the receiver some cover because you asked her for her opinion, she might be more likely to give you an answer. The fear is of course, if you are injudicious, you could end up asking the arrogant and incompetent who will lead you astray. It is a powerful question and if you do use it, prepare the situation so it can be properly received. The rest of this chapter will address preparing the situation so this type of question can be well received.

The Sequencing Process
As important as asking clarifying questions is explicitly making the connection between the information and your counteroffer. I discovered that if I, as the mediator, put the information in the right order, the receiver would respond favorably. Later, I began teaching this method and my training and coaching clients also had favorable responses.

Step One – Ask the question. The first step is to ask the clarifying question, or questions. Let's say that you think that you would like to agree to their requested price reduction if they would agree to reduce the warranty period on your widget. Rather than making an assumption that this is agreeable, test it with a question such as, "what is the least important thing you need from us?" The next step is to verify their answer.

Step Two – Restate their response. This step is an important step. People won't give you all the information you need or they might give you pieces of the information. Let's say in this scenario that your counterpart tells you that customer support is the least important thing. First of all, this is good to know because you might have assumed that customer support was very important. Secondly, you need to understand what he means by customer support. You might say something like, "If I understand you correctly, you are saying that all of our 24/7 support is not important to you?" You are not parroting back the statement but making sure that you really are talking about the same thing. The last thing you want to do is eliminate all customer support from your proposal just to later learn that the customer meant your company's in-person support was not necessary but your company's telephone support was necessary.

Usually, a person will respond in one of two ways. They will agree and you move on to the next step, or they might say that's not what they meant. In that case, you go back to your clarifying questions to ask them what they mean by customer support et cetera. Remember, you are very curious at this point, particularly if you are surprised by the response.

Step Three – Make the counteroffer. Assuming that you are correct, that your counterpart believes that your customer support is not very important to him use that response to make your counteroffer. It might sound like this, "Since you are not interested in our 24/7 customer support, we would be willing to agree to the price reduction you requested. So, in exchange for eliminating 24/7 customer support from the package, we will reduce our price by 10%."

This counteroffer is more likely to meet with approval for three very important reasons. One, you asked them what--from their perspective-they found least important. You also verified this information to make sure that you both were talking about the same thing. Two, you clearly made the connection between what they said and your offer. Three, you made your offer contingent on their willingness to give something up. Now, your counterpart has a clear picture about what is at play and that the conversation is a give and take.

Notice that not once in this example did you ever talk about what you cannot do for your customer. They don't care why you cannot reduce the price by 15%, or change the delivery schedule or whatever you are worried about. Increasingly, customers care about making sure that their supplier can get the job done with minimal oversight. If you must have a discussion about what you cannot do for your counterpart, make it a separate conversation from the counteroffer conversation.

Let's say that you cannot separate customer service from the package price for whatever reason. Rather than saying, "we can't do that" and then making a counteroffer to reduce the warranty period as you originally intended, have a full conversation about customer service. Take time to understand what service they provide internally. Then put on the teacher hat to explain how customer service

> **Increasingly, customers care about making sure that their supplier can get the job done with minimal oversight.**

is integral to the contract. If possible, delay the counteroffer about the warranty to another time by asking them to do some research or to talk to someone about some issue. If that is not feasible, and sometimes it is not, find a way to make the counteroffer seem like a different conversation. Make a clear break from the negative conversation about what you cannot do to the positive conversation about what you can do.

There are still two elements to consider in this counterproposal process: How you should time the counterproposal and how you should deliver it. These elements are just as critical as gathering information and pitching it the right way.

Timing
By timing I mean the pace at which you make the counteroffer. Do you present the supporting information first or do you make the counteroffer first followed by the supporting information? There is no one right way, only considerations that may influence you one way or another. I've coached clients to time counteroffers using both methods. In fact, there may be other methods in addition to these two. The important factor is to understand the reasoning behind each decision.

Long Lead In. In this method, my client chose to present a lot of supporting, factual information before actually making the counteroffer. Because the negotiations were about the valuation of a thriving business, there was a lot of financial information that the sellers wanted the buyers to consider. The sellers wanted to marry price and value in one conversation. The sellers felt that by laying out all of the information first, there would be less likelihood of the conversation going off track when the buyer heard the counterproposal. Before choosing this method, the sellers had several exploratory conversations with the buyers after which the buyers made the opening offer. Therefore, the sellers had a feel for what the buyers considered important and relied on those indicators throughout the counteroffer conversation. At the very end of the presentation of the facts, the sellers made their counteroffer. When the buyers showed signs of balking at the counteroffer price, the sellers asked a clarifying question, "what's your concern with our counteroffer?" The response was not what the sellers anticipated. It was not about the price per se. Their concern was about getting approval for that price range from those higher up in the organization, which was easily solved by providing all the supporting information and calculations. Three months later, the sellers closed the deal and announced the merger to the business community.

Just Get To It. In this method, a different client decided to do the opposite of the client mentioned above. In this situation, my client had negotiated for three months to reach an agreement on all the terms of the deal. There were lengthy email exchanges and both companies made numerous tradeoffs and counteroffers until the deal was ready to be reviewed by the customer's legal department. My client received an alarming call from legal alerting her that there was no deal unless her company significantly reduced the price. My client was—for very good reasons—completely unwilling to make another price reduction.

After some consideration, we decided that my client's counterproposal would be that the customer would have to be willing to make a tradeoff before my client would discuss price again. My client chose to start the conversation with the fact that her company was not making a price concession but was open to receiving a tradeoff. The conversation then went from there to various aspects of the contract that had been discussed and a request that the customer consider offering something in return for the price reduction it was seeking. My client felt that had she presented all of the information about why her company was unwilling to concede this issue, the impact of her counterproposal would have been lost. This way, she reasoned, the customer would recognize that her company was not conceding price.

Choosing a timing method depends on the circumstances. Are you negotiating via email? In that case, you want to be more thoughtful about the language you use and the placement of the counterproposal. If you put it upfront, your counterpart might not read your reasoning, and simply reply, "no." It's happened. Are you negotiating with the decision maker? If not, you want to educate the representatives so that they are comfortable taking your message back to the decision maker. You don't want them to feel embarrassed that they could not answer their bosses' questions. What message do you want to send? Are you signaling a willingness to meet their needs, or do you need to hold the line and call their bluff? All of these considerations also lead to the final element in structuring counteroffers – how do you deliver the message?

> **Studies show that 93% of all communication is transmitted non-verbally.**

Delivering the Counteroffer

As I've mentioned, this is an increasingly electronic world. Email is a bane and a boon to our working life. It sucks mental energy while simultaneously allowing us to easily share volumes of information instantaneously. There are advantages and disadvantages to meeting face to face too. One disadvantage is that there can be pressure to get a deal inked. Because so much time and effort went into scheduling the face to face meeting, many feel that they have to have something tangible to show for it. On the other hand, nothing replaces the negotiator's ability to read between the lines than looking your counterpart in the eye. Studies show that 93% of all communication is transmitted non-verbally. That means that you convey messages about the deal in your facial expressions, your body gestures and the tone of your voice. None of this is communicated via email. Let's face reality, emoticons are silly and never convey the same message that a sincere smile or a frown conveys. What should you do?

The first thing you need to realize is that you must work effectively with what ever delivery method you choose. If you have used email and phone calls to bargain back and forth to this point, then you may choose email. If you do, make accommodations for its limitations (doesn't convey any non-verbal information) and leverage its strengths (easy medium for conveying a lot of information). If you want to have a web based meeting, plan it. Don't wing it. Have an agenda and stick to it. People get squirrely if conversations are not to the point. They might even be like me, check out and start emailing people while the meeting drags on. If you really want to close the deal, meet face to face and be prepared to use the leverage of the in-person meeting to get an agreement. That may mean having all your ducks in a row so your counterpart cannot claim to need information before agreeing to your counterproposal. What ever you do choose, be conscious and deliberate. It will save you and your company, time, money and aggravation.

Bottom line, unsuccessful negotiators must recognize what the successful negotiators already know: Deliberate actions pay huge dividends at the bargaining table.

Do not leave counteroffers to chance. Negotiators of all stripes will tell you war stories about negotiations gone south. Many times, there was an element of surprise which helped move the negotiations off track. The best way you can control the situation when you are making a counterproposal is to carefully structure it. That means taking the time to think about the elements outlined in this chapter. Don't tell yourself you don't have the time. You always have time to make more money and what could be easier than making more money by making a successful counteroffer? Deliberate actions pay huge dividends at the bargaining table.

Chapter Seven

............................▶

Appropriately Using Leverage

Acquiring and using leverage is the most reliable way to make sure that you achieve your goals at any bargaining session. Leverage is not just your power to walk away: It is your power to obtain an agreement on your own terms.[1] In other words, true leverage is getting what you want, when you want it and how you want it. You may think that others, especially large companies, have leverage and you do not. But, think again. Everyone, and I mean everyone, has some leverage.

Unsuccessful negotiators face three issues when managing leverage at the bargaining table. The first and most significant problem is that they don't know that they have any leverage at all. This lack of insight creates an outward looking, hat-in-hand stance that signals weakness to their counterpart. That stance leads directly to the second problem. Too often unsuccessful negotiators succumb to their counterpart's false claims that they have all the leverage. This most often plays itself out

Acquiring and using leverage is the most reliable way to make sure that you achieve your goals at any bargaining session.

in the form of threats that the counterpart will walk away from the deal. When managed properly, those threats lose their sting and become just another tactic to be dealt with. Finally, the third problem is an unwillingness by unsuccessful negotiators to use the leverage to their advantage. Luckily, all three problems can be easily addressed.

Successful negotiators intuitively understand the need to use leverage and have tools in place to limit the other party's overreliance on negative leverage. By reading and applying the tools in this chapter, you will understand the different forms of leverage, know how to assess leverage and understand how to appropriately use leverage to your advantage.

Combine and Alter

Appropriately using leverage is one's ability to balance needs and fears at the bargaining table. You and the other party will have some common needs, some individual needs, and some opposing needs. Likewise, you and the other party will have some shared fears, some individual fears and some opposing fears. Let's use an example to illustrate this point. Imagine that you are a small manufacturer supplying a Fortune 1000 company. One common need would be customer satisfaction. For the small manufacturer, an individual need might be accurate forecasting. One opposing need might be price, as your idea and their idea of a fair price could be at odds.

You can likewise use this example to talk about fears. One common fear might be leaving money on the table. For the Fortune 1000 company, one individual fear might be an inability on the small manufacturer's part to fulfill the contract. One opposing fear might be walking away from the deal, as the impact of walking away from the table might affect the Fortune 1000 company differently than your company.

Two goals can be achieved when successfully using leverage. One goal is to combine different types of leverage into a seamless package. For example, in a tough negotiation it is not enough to show the other party that you can deliver what the other party wants and needs. You must also persuade the other party that she has something to lose if the negotiations fall through. The other goal is to use this package to alter the situation so that you have less to lose than the other side.

Since one goal for using leverage is to combine different forms of leverage into a package, it is important to understand the three different types of leverage. By type, I mean a negotiator's ability to label the leverage so its impact at the bargaining table is easily identifiable.

Positive Leverage

The most overlooked and undervalued form of leverage is positive leverage. Positive leverage is having what the other party wants, needs, or — best of all — cannot live without. Depending on what your company's business is, positive leverage can range from quality, to innovation, to speed. I suggest that when combining leverage into a package, you always include some form of positive leverage.

At training and coaching sessions, I often hear comments that suggest that positive leverage is not as important as negative leverage when negotiating a deal. This is not true. In fact, positive leverage is incredibly important precisely because its appropriate use means that your counterpart is getting what it most wants from the deal. To overlook this is akin to overlooking your company's value proposition in the market.

Negative Leverage

Negative leverage, whether openly discussed or merely hinted at, looms large at most negotiation sessions. Humans are psychology programmed to fear losing something they perceive as valuable, even if they don't actually possess that thing. Many unsuccessful negotiators have told me that they

Business to business negotiations are multi-layer, multi-dimensional transactions that have a lasting impact on both businesses beyond the bargaining table.

must make concessions in order to not lose a deal. This stands the entire deal making process on its head. Rather than looking at the deal from the perspective of what they must offer to get the deal, they focus on not losing the deal. Because the threat of losing something is more powerful in the human mind than gaining something, these negotiators quickly succumb to the other party's threats.

The fact of the matter is that most negative leverage is illusory at best. Most businesses don't really have a viable option other than the one your company offers[2], nor do they really have a competitor of yours waiting in the wings ready to take your business away. They tell you that your competitor will beat your price to induce you to drop your price below that set by your competitor. They use the fear of loss to motivate your actions to their benefit.

I interviewed two small privately owned businesses in the Pacific Northwest who rose above negative leverage by allowing Fortune 500 companies to walk away from the deal, as they had promised to do if the small companies did not lower their prices. In both instances, the large companies walked away from the bargaining table and in both circumstances, the large companies were back at the bargaining table within months making deals with the small companies on the small companies' terms. Not only did the large companies have no viable alternatives, their bluffs were called. Both small company owners reported to me that they were very gracious at their customers' return to the table. It's easy to understand why: they now had more leverage than did their customers.

Successful negotiators who really have powerful leverage—the ability to not lose anything if the deal is not done–carefully use negative leverage. They understand that business to business negotiations are multi-layer, multi-dimensional transactions that have a lasting impact on both businesses beyond the bargaining table. For that reason alone, they use negative leverage judiciously and wisely.

Normative Leverage

The last type of leverage is normative leverage. Normative leverage is based on the negotiators individual desire to act consistently with their values, or to act consistently with shared values.[3] In other words, negotiators will act consistently with values that they themselves determine to be legitimate and relevant. For example, publicly traded companies all live and die by Wall Street's analysis of their quarterly performance. Adherence to this system is one form of normative leverage for publicly traded companies. Because it is deemed legitimate and relevant, a skilled merger negotiator could use adherence to Wall Street as a form of normative leverage to ensure that the deal is equitable for both companies, lest it be criticized by Wall Street imperiling both companies share prices.

When using normative leverage, frame needs as principles and norms that both companies strive to live by. Every company wants to make enough money to stay in business. Likewise, companies want their customers and vendors to stay in business. Framing a conversation as "We're all in the same game together" is a form of normative leverage. I find that when a negotiator accurately determines what normative leverage will most resonate with their counterpart, and then combines that leverage with positive leverage, the deal is arrived at quickly. It works because framing the deal upon principles that the other party respects while also giving them what they want is hard to turn down.

Utilizing different types of leverage to alter the situation and create an advantage is only one part of the equation. The other part is your ability to accurately assess who has leverage at any given moment. When you can accurately assess leverage, you will use your own leverage more appropriately and strike better deals more quickly.

Leverage is dynamic. It can and will change at a moments notice.

Assessing Leverage-Who Has It?

Because leverage is dynamic, you need a quick way to asses leverage in the moment. When assessing leverage, you need to ask yourself two key questions. The first question is, "who controls the status quo?"[4]   Usually, those who control the status quo have greater leverage. Status quo means preserving something. In business, the status quo is dictated by any contract between your company and another company.

Some unsuccessful negotiators fall into the trap of thinking that they have to cave in to every demand that their customers make of them without assessing the situation. If your company has a contract with another company and the other company calls to demand a change, your company may have leverage. The one seeking to change the contract actually has less leverage than she realizes. Because the status quo is abiding by the contract and many contracts dictate how changes are made, if at all, your leverage may arise from the contractual provisions that don't allow unilateral modifications.

Successful negotiators, on the other hand, use the customer's request as an opportunity to exert leverage by simultaneously negotiating another provision of the contract while granting the customers request. A customer told my client of mine that it would no longer pay its bills within 30 days, as established within the contract. It would pay within 45 days. That meant that my client was acting like a bank for 15 days. What the customer did not realize was the discount they received was tied to timely payment. Rather than caving to their demand, my client told the customer that the discount no longer applied. The customer was stunned. It was not prepared for this response. The status quo was the fact that the discount was contractually tied to timely payments. Therefore, my client had the leverage to discontinue the discount if the customer did not pay its bills on time. After some negotiating, both my client and its customer got what they needed. My client cut the discount in half and extended the payment terms to 45 days. Without an understanding that my client had leverage, they would not have been able to negotiate a reduction in the discount to make up for the extension in credit.

As can be seen from the following example, controlling the status quo doesn't mean the other side is without leverage. Employees who have a better offer from another company have a lot of leverage with their current employer, yet they do not control the status quo. The employer controls the working relationship and in many states can fire employees without cause. But, if an employee has a better job offer and uses that offer to negotiate a better salary with her current employer, the balance of needs and fears has shifted to favor the employee. This example illustrates the second question you must also ask yourself when assessing leverage.

Successful negotiators intuitively understand the need to use leverage and have tools in place to limit the other party's overreliance on negative leverage.

Assessing Leverage-Who Has the Most to Lose?

This question helps give fuller depth to the first assessment question. "As of the moment when you make the assessment, which party has the most to lose from not making a deal?"[5] The party with the most to lose has the least leverage; the party with the least to lose has the most leverage; and both parties have roughly equal leverage when they both stand to lose equivalent amounts should the deal fall through.[6]

This is a critical question. Because circumstances change in the course of a long negotiation, one party could suddenly find itself in a situation in which it now has more to lose from not reaching an agreement than it did, say, two months ago. Several of my clients have faced this situation in varying degrees. One case though illustrates this point well.

A software engineering company was engaged in some protracted licensing negotiations with a much larger company. After several months, my client and the purchasing agent came to an agreement, which was documented in a series of emails. Once the agreement went to my client's opponent for legal review, my client got a startling call—no deal. The licensing fee was too much. My client pulled several people together for an emergency conference call with the potential customer. During the call, my client requested several days to consider proposed changes to the pricing structure. The lawyer for the other side asked the purchasing agent at his own company (in front of my client so to speak) "how will this delay impact our development schedule?" Leverage just shifted giving my client more leverage than it had only one hour earlier. My client now knew the potential customer was committed to licensing the software because they had already established a project schedule for integrating and rolling out the software. When assessing this conversation the question concerning who had the most to lose revealed that the potential customer had more to lose than my client if the deal fell through.

Everyone has some type of leverage at some point during the negotiation session. It might come from an insistence on adherence to the contract, or from a blunder at the bargaining table. Nevertheless, recognition of leverage and a willingness to use it meant that two seemingly disadvantaged companies reached an agreement on good terms.

Successful negotiators do two things really well. First, they spend time thinking about all three forms of leverage: Positive, negative and normative. While some leverage points might be easy for you to recognize ("We have the innovation your company has been searching for!"), take time to look for the other more subtle leverage points. Think about how to use shared interests to your advantage. Consider the norms or shared principles you both strive to live by. These leverage points may be less obvious than the example of positive leverage, it is none the less a very powerful form of leverage.

Second, successful negotiators are constantly assessing the situation to determine who has leverage and who has the most to lose from not reaching a deal at that moment. Because leverage is dynamic, you must assess leverage throughout the negotiation, not just at the beginning. After all, the situation could change and you must be ready to take advantage of it, or risk losing your chance all together.

Leverage is your ability to strike a deal on your own terms. Successful negotiators spend time assessing and appropriately using their leverage. This is simply the most reliable way to make sure that you achieve your goals at any bargaining session.

Chapter Eight

........................▶

Balancing Power at the Bargaining Table

Power plays an important role in the negotiation process. As it relates to the bargaining process, power is your ability to alter other people's attitudes and behaviors. People react to power in many different ways. If your counterpart reacts to your power in a way that gets you more of what you want, you have fulfilled your intention to bring about a certain outcome. If your counterpart reacts in ways that hinder your ability to get more of what you want, you are not powerful, and may have unwittingly shifted the power to the other party.

There are many misperceptions about power that tremendously impact the negotiation process. Unsuccessful negotiators don't recognize their power, or avoid using their power. Many of my clients often think that they don't have any power. This belief puts them at a disadvantage when working with those who know that they represent a seemingly powerful entity.

Successful negotiators understand the role that power plays at the bargaining table.

Then there are the negotiators who openly abuse their power, or abuse their company's standing by bullying their counterpart. Often times, these bullies create a distrust of their entire organization and an enmity that far exceeds the confines of the bargaining table. This is the abuse of power.

Successful negotiators understand the role that power plays at the bargaining table. They learn when to temper their power, or what tools to use to help them level the playing field. By understanding and accepting power as an important aspect of the bargaining process, they are less likely to be bullied into accepting unfair deals or inappropriately imposing unfair deals.

After reading this chapter, you will have a better grasp of the role that power really plays at the bargaining table, including sources of power. You will also learn the mistakes that self-professed powerful negotiators make at the bargaining table. Finally, you will have tools to help you level the playing field, even if you think that you don't have any power, so that you no longer feel intimidated by your counterpart.

Two Perspectives on Power

There are two primary perspectives on power. One is that power will be used to dominate and control the other person, company or entity. And frankly, the lack of control is most companies' greatest fear. It does not matter whether it is a small company or a large company business people dislike a lack of control. Small companies specifically fear being overrun by a big company's demands, while larger companies fear being held hostage by a supplier that cannot deliver.

Bill Lincoln, an accomplished international mediator famous for bringing mediators to war torn countries from the former Soviet Union to Afghanistan, once said, "Hunting mice with an elephant gun is not power it is the abuse of power."[1] While this quip is quite illustrative, it is also quite true. We often assume that all uses of power are bad, when in fact what we are talking about is the abuse of power. Those times when one person, company or entity uses its power in such a way as to harm another person, company or entity are examples of the abuse of power.

The other, and far less discussed, perspective on power is the power to bring people together for a common solution. That power is often used in more subtle ways, and in fact is overlooked by negotiators. Mediators, whether professionally certified or those unofficial good souls who always seem to smooth things over between disgruntled teams, organizations or companies, frequently use this more subtle form of power to achieve their aim. While there is an upside to using dominance to bring people together, being on the receiving end of an in artful power play can leave people, companies and organizations feeling bitter, resentful and cynical. If you find yourself on the downside of a power play there are steps you can take to help level the playing field.

> **The other, and far less discussed, perspective on power is the power to bring people together for a common solution.**

Leveling the Playing Field

I've been asked many times, "What should I do if I'm less powerful than my counterpart?" There are several immediate steps to take to level the playing field. First, be willing to use your power. Those negotiators who believe that they are less powerful fail to recognize their own sources of power, and if they do recognize them, fail to use them. They fail to use them for three reasons. First, they think that they will have to go toe-to-toe with their counterpart. Second, they don't know how the other party will react so they do nothing. Third, they are not sure how they will react under the pressure created by using power, so they do nothing.

Another step you can take is to recognize your source of power. There are five recognized sources of power. Looking at the five sources of power listed below, which source can you immediately draw on?

Information. The first source of power is your ability to accumulate, use or withhold information. In my experience, withholding vital information is the most destructive source of power. I've seen disputes on the verge of settling disintegrate as one person ever so casually informs the other of some secret information that is meant to derail the deal. Not only does withholding vital information damage trust it permanently hinders the negotiating process itself.

Personality. Another source of power is personality. Charismatic leaders wield a lot of power by sheer force of their personality. The downside to this source of power is using their personality to make issues a righteous cause, rather than a rational disagreement between adults of varying perspectives. Righteousness also clouds people's ability to recognize and accept reasonable solutions to a problem.

Title or Position. Your position whether at your company or at the bargaining table is yet another source of power. In a hierarchy, people naturally defer to the person of highest rank. This deference can easily be abused by those who hold a specific title, causing ill-will and distrust. It is worth noting that in other cultures, power associated with title is more prevalent than it is here in the United States.

Network. People who are great networkers, both inside of the company and in the greater community in which they live have a source of power. These people have access to information (a source of power), people and resources as a result of their active participation in a network. George Clooney's character Michael Clayton is an obvious example of this source of power. Clooney's character is valued by the firm for his ability to fix things, and he can only fix things when he has a broad and responsive network.

Context. Contextual power is the final source of power. Contextual power represents those times when a negotiator has a strong alternative to a negotiated agreement (**BATNA**), a powerful constituency or an attentive audience. These attributes can be fleeting and when present should be used in a timely manner. An example of contextual power might be a striking teacher's union who has the parents' sympathies and the public's attention. For the few days that teachers are on strike talking about getting classroom resources and a two-dollar an hour raise, the parents, students and community at are drawn into the discussion. This type of contextual power may not last long. Tides of public opinion can turn on a dime leaving the other party with the contextual power.

Next, take an honest look at the other person's source of power. What are they relying on for their source of power? In the Wizard of Oz, Dorothy only went home after she realized that all the things that frightened her were more the making of her imagination than reality. Moreover, research shows that self professed powerful negotiators suffer from their own illusions; illusions that you can penetrate if you are observant.

A study revealed[2] that self-professed powerful negotiators suffer from one great illusion. They think that they are smarter than the underdog. In fact, research shows that self-professed powerful negotiators don't gather data, ineffectively use the data that they do have, and use simplistic analysis to reach conclusions. I've also personally found that self-professed powerful negotiators make these mistakes.

This study should give you hope if you are the underdog. Your source of power ought to be information and its use throughout the negotiation process. This is the quickest and most effective way to level the playing field. Take time to create an advantage by gathering data, analyzing data and then create a strategy to effectively use your data throughout the negotiations. My belief is that I cannot control my counterpart, but I can control how much information I posses. In fact, this attitude significantly improved the bargaining position of one of my clients.

A large company approached my client, a small start-up, wanting to purchase it. The large company did not posture or present itself as being dominant. Nevertheless, my client wanted to feel as if it were on a level playing field. Their solution was to be thoroughly prepared for all conversations, and in fact, had a better grasp of the information than the larger company had. When making presentations about their company to the larger company, they were keenly aware that their knowledge placed them on equal footing.

Finally, when meeting a power imbalance, do what you can to create an advantage where none existed before. One powerful way to mitigate power imbalances is to combine positive and normative leverage with shared interests when making offers and counteroffers. Rather than reacting to their power plays, step back, be proactive and create an advantage for yourself. Ask yourself a series of questions like,

- What do you have that they cannot live without?
- What values or common goals do you both share?
- What common vision for the future can you leverage?

These questions will help you think about ways you can create an advantage.

Power in and of itself is not bad. It is the abuse of power that you want to avoid; using power to destroy, demean or damage ought to be avoided at the bargaining table. If you find yourself on the receiving end of the misuse of power, there are ways that you can level that playing field. Look for ways to use data more effectively. You might also balance the playing field by conscientiously using positive and normative leverage. And finally, don't be afraid to use your sources of power.

Remember this: It takes far more energy to fight against than it does to work towards.

Research shows that self-professed powerful negotiators don't gather data, ineffectively use the data that they do have, and use simplistic analysis to reach conclusions.

Many people don't initially realize it, but if you talk to business men and women about the relationships that seem to work best through thick and thin, it is those relationships that work for rather than those that work against.

Chapter Nine

......................................➤

Influential Power at the Bargaining Table

As a successful negotiator you must be able to influence your counterpart. Without the power to influence, you run the risk of being manipulated and pressured into agreeing to terms that are not as favorable as you'd like. Influence is your ability to persuade your counterpart to see things from your perspective, which will allow you both to feel as though you both have reached a favorable agreement.

Influence is far more subtle than dominate power. One specific aspect of influence, messaging, is the easiest way for any unskilled negotiator to develop influence. Developing influence by framing the content, articulating and pitching your message is not dependant on any external source of power, nor is it dependant on your personality. It is dependant on your ability to listen carefully to what is and is not being said, while at the same time carefully considering how and what you will say to your counterpart.

Successful negotiators are by their nature and training influential.

Successful negotiators are by their nature and training influential. They spend more time than average negotiators thinking about how to frame and pitch their messages. Successful negotiators take into consideration things like, who will be hearing the message, how to best frame the message and how to best pitch that message. Moreover, successful negotiators spend time gathering information and then use that information to explicitly address their counterpart's needs and concerns. The end result is successful negotiators get their counterpart to discuss issues, to engage in problem solving and to acknowledge common ground, all of which leads to reasonable agreements.

Unsuccessful negotiators, on the other hand, make a series of common mistakes which reduce their influence at the bargaining table. First, unsuccessful negotiators tend to frame their conversations from a self-serving perspective. Understandably, all negotiations are self-serving, but successful negotiators tend to invite their counterpart to look at things differently, rather than force a perspective on their counterpart. It is all a matter of how the message is framed and pitched. Moreover, unsuccessful negotiators miss an important point: It's your job at the bargaining table to articulate what your counterpart has to gain from following your proposed course of action. When you spend time spinning things from your company's perspective, you ruin all chances at positively influencing your counterpart. Your counterpart is thinking about his company's bottom line, his deadlines, and his purchasing routine. Your failure to address his concerns at the bargaining table means he is on his own when it comes to meeting his needs and solving his concerns.

Second, and related to the first mistake, unsuccessful negotiators don't craft their message; they simply say whatever comes to mind. There are more stories, funny and sad, about people saying whatever comes to mind while at the bargaining table. Unsuccessful negotiators also miss opportunities to turn conversations around.

Third, unsuccessful negotiators don't understand persuasive nature of messages and therefore don't use them effectively. They think that power point slides, complicated proposals or free incentives will send an effective message and persuade their counterpart to go their way. They don't use messages about meeting everyone's needs or leveraging common ground to help persuade the other party.

By reading this chapter, you will have useful and practical tools for enhancing your influence. You will learn how to control the messages you send to your counterpart by considering different aspects of message content. You will understand what it means to make a message attractive. You will also have the tools to turn a conversation around so your counterpart is more likely to see things from your perspective. Finally, you will have a better understanding of frames and how framing messages can help you be more effective.

One specific aspect of influence, messaging, is the easiest way for any unskilled negotiator to develop influence.

There are different aspects to message content. Each is important in its own right, but not all may be applicable to your negotiation. The key to using content as an influential tool is to ensure that the other party fully understands what it will gain from your solution, proposal, offer to settle or whatever you are seeking agreement on. It is surprising to me how often negotiators fail to explain in plain and clear terms what the other party has to gain from a certain course of action.

Make the Message More Attractive

The first rule of messaging is to make the information, data, proposal, offer to settle, or solution attractive to the other side. It is simple enough, and rarely done. An attractive message is one that attempts to meet your counterpart's needs or address some concern. Your solution, request or proposal should explicitly tell your counterpart that you've heard them and that by agreeing to your proposal or suggestion, they will meet their needs or address their concerns. As a skilled negotiator, you cannot leave it to chance that your counterpart will figure out how your proposal or suggestion will meet her needs.

The second rule of messaging is to make complex information simple. Do this even if you think that they should understand the complexity. Don't assume that they will understand. Many people don't want to look stupid and won't let on that they are not following you. Additionally, in a complex sale, the negotiation team has to take proposals to others in the organization who are not seated at the bargaining table. Understanding the message in the context is not the same as being able to convey the message to someone else. Make it easy for someone to carry your message forward. Break it down for them, but be careful not to insinuate that they are stupid or it will backfire on you.

The third rule of messaging is to use information to craft a message that speaks to their specific needs, wants and desires while meeting your own needs at the same time. For example, you might start a conversation by acknowledging that your counterpart is concerned about price and delivery. In order to meet these two needs, your suggestion might be to reach an agreement on a forecasting method that will allow your company to buy larger quantities of commodities at a discount while at the same time passing along the price break to your customer. This scenario tells the customer that you've considered its concerns, while at the same time you are addressing your own concerns. You do not go on about how your company cannot agree to a price cut because your company never knows how much raw materials it needs, and doesn't want to buy high at the last minute. Talking all about what you cannot do is not attractive or influential to your customer.

The fourth rule of messaging is leveraging common ground. Have you ever heard people start conversations with sentences like, "You know Bob, we both believe in getting a fair price for the widget." The speaker is leveraging the shared interest of paying for and receiving a fair price. This kind of common ground is universal. In this example, the common ground is fairness. How the speaker and listener continue to define fairness can bring them both together rather than push them apart. It is important for you as a skillful negotiator to recognize and leverage common ground or shared motivations. Once you recognize those areas, explicitly talk about them with your counterpart. My experience has proven that people respond well to discussions about common ground and shared motivations.

The fifth and final rule of messaging is active listening. In order to know what will make a particular message attractive to your counterpart is having a clear picture of their needs and concerns. You have to subtly and artfully uncover their hidden motivations before you can address them. The active listening skills that I learned as a mediator have proved very useful for business to business negotiations.

Active Listening

I learned as mediator to make messages more attractive by applying some simple active listening techniques. I was surprised at how well they worked until I realized how often people talk as if their counterpart was not even part of the process. I've seen negotiators spend so much time fretting about their own wants and needs, and defending their own positions to the bitter end, that I could have put a cardboard cut-out in their counterpart's chair and no one would have noticed the difference!

Active listening sends a signal that you understand your counterpart's needs and concerns. That's all. It doesn't mean that you will sacrifice your needs to meet their needs. It just means that you hear what the other party is concerned about. By really listening to your counterpart, you pave the way to a more fruitful back and forth conversation. You can demonstrate to your counterpart that you heard what she just said and that your proposal, offer, or suggestion takes into consideration your counterpart's needs and concerns. It also allows both of to further clarify what you are talking about by unearthing hidden motivations.

Active listening sends a signal that you understand your counterpart's needs and concerns. That's all.

Here is a three step process that I use. I make sure that when I use this process, I am genuine. If you cannot be genuine, don't use this technique; you will only make matters worse by looking like you are mocking your counterpart.

Step One – Repeat the statement. When I am trying to understand where someone is coming from, I make sure that I repeat the statement, whether it is a need, want, concern or a demand. I don't parrot the other party. I simply state what I've heard. I've learned that because people talk without thinking at the bargaining table, they often say things that don't make sense or assume that I have information that I actually don't have.

When I am repeating something, I use certain phrases like, "if I understand what you are saying, . ." or "correct me if I'm wrong, . . ." Then, depending on the complexity of the information, I will either paraphrase the statement or repeat it back almost word for word. Because I am genuinely curious, people confirm, or correct me, and often elaborate on what they mean.

Step Two – Ask clarifying questions. Next, I follow up with some questions that are intended to get the other party talking about what is important to them. I use some open ended questions to help draw out my counterpart. I also shut up and listen to what the other party has to say. I see so many instances where someone will ask a question and then keep talking never allowing the other person to actually answer the question. I also see people ask really pointed questions. These pointed questions, like "you'd agree with me that keeping the warranty is important," can cause a defensive reaction. Here are nine clarifying questions and one statement. (The same ten listed in Chapter 6.)

- What is your greatest concern with . . . ?
- What bothers you the most about that suggestion?
- What about . . . . is important to you?
- Tell me more about . . . . .
- What does . . . look like to you?
- How can we make our proposal fit your need to {spell their need and/or interest out}?
- What is the most/least important thing you need from us?
- How important is . . . to the overall picture?
- How do you see that we can accomplish . . .?
- If you were in my shoes, what would you recommend?

Step Three – Reframe the answer in a positive light. Finally, I reframe their answers to the clarifying questions in a positive way. While the other person is talking, I listen for positive motivations. I then weave those motivations into my statement. As I mentioned in earlier chapters, most people, and almost all business people, are motivated by positive concerns. It's just that at the bargaining table, people assume that their needs must be pitted against someone else's needs. It is in this light that their wants and concerns appear to be negative to you.

To help demonstrate the influential nature of this process, let me give you an example from my career as an attorney. I cannot give you the verbatim exchange, but I can give you a flavor of how I used the process. Here is some background information.

My client hired me specifically for my mediation skills, but rather than mediate, I advocated for my client's interests. My client, an association, hired a contractor as an expert to evaluate some poor workmanship on a building and to make the necessary repairs. The parties quickly became at odds with one another. There were cost overruns and disagreements about authority to proceed on work that exceeded the scope of the contract. As tensions mounted, the contractor became irascible and combative (As a note, the contractor insisted he didn't want his lawyer involved). When I entered the picture, the contractor was threatening to sue my client.

In this exchange, I wanted to start talking about the scope of the project. The contractor was so angry that my goal was just to tone down the rhetoric so that we have a more reasonable conversation about settling the disagreement.

Contractor: *Your client is a liar. If they don't pay this by the 21st I'll file a lawsuit against them in court. In fact, that's what I should have done two months ago when I gave them the final invoice.*

Me: *I understand you want to be paid.* (This is step one. I simply paraphrased what I heard. I've not acknowledged the liar part or admitted that my client owed him anything.)

Contractor: *Damn right. I'm angry. Your client signed a contract and agreed to pay my company. If they told you they didn't agree to the work, they're a bunch of liars and I should just sue them.*

Me: *I have the contract in front of me. I need to ask you some questions.*

Contractor: *So you see then that they signed it and agreed to pay my company for the work that I did?* (This is a trap. It is a pointed question which will lead to defensive angry words being exchanged. The contractor wants me to admit to something that he knows I do not agree with. My message to you is that it is unwise to ask these types of questions if you are trying to influence your counterpart in any way.)

Me: *I see that it was a "not to exceed" contract. Can you tell me about how the bills came to be more than double the quoted price?* (This is step two. I am using a clarifying question in connection with the fact that the contract was a "not to exceed" contract.)

The contractor then went into a lengthy discussion about the work that had been done and all of the phone calls and emails to my client about the problems at the job site. When he finished, I reframed the conversation.

Me: *Ok. So from your perspective, if my client had a problem with the cost overruns, they should have told you to stop working on the project and tell you that they had no intention of paying you for the extra work.* (This is step three, the reframe of the liar part of his earlier statement. It is not positive, just neutral. Rather than having a conversation about lying, I was starting to talk more neutrally about what was said in those phone calls. Not once did I admit my client lied, had an obligation to do anything, or agree that my client did anything wrong. I did signal to the contractor that I heard from his perspective why he felt frustrated. He never again accused my client of being a liar.)

Contractor: *That's right.*

Me: *It looks like my client did tell you in an email that they were concerned about the project and wanted you to tell them before the next board meeting how much of the deposit you had used so far.*

In all of my conversations with this man, I made sure that I acknowledged what he had said before I made my point. I also used the information that he gave me, like the fact that there were phone calls and email exchanges, to help him see that my client had raised concerns about the scope of the work, and once the work was done tried to put a payment plan in place.

This exchange is influence in action. I was making my message more attractive by not pitting his anger against my client's rights, and I was using this listening technique to look for and leverage common ground. In this way, I was changing his story from liar/victim to a negotiated settlement about cost overruns. In the end after a couple of months of negotiations, my client and the contractor settled on a final payment amount.

In addition to making the content of any message attractive and listening to your counterpart, you must also be able to pitch a message. By pitching a message, I mean you must be able to put a frame around it. A frame implies how the message should be interpreted.

Pitch the Message by Framing the Conversation

There is an old adage in law: He who frames the issue wins the argument. Frames are a mechanism through which people evaluate and make sense of situations.[1] Successful negotiators choose to frame the issue in a way that will allow their counterpart to better hear the issue. Meaning, a skilled negotiator will recognize the most appropriate frame and place the message, solution or offer in that frame.

For example, say you are a sales person meeting with the CFO at a midsized company. The end user of your service is the HR department but they don't negotiate the "fine print", the CFO does. You can be fairly certain that that CFO will have a different frame of reference as the financial buyer than the HR department will have as the end user of your services. The CFO will be looking at the bottom line and how much your services cost, and may think your services cost too much. While the primary concern for the HR department will be outlining the precise scope of the project and ensuring that you make good on your promises that your services will quickly address their pressing issues. This is not to say that the CFO is not interested in your services or that HR is unimpressed with budget concerns. It means that you will frame your message to the CFO differently than to the HR department. Assuming that you will give the same pitch to both is unwise. It is important to know that each buyer in this scenario has a certain lens that they are accustomed to looking through, and any attempt on your part to get them to use a different lens will fail.

There are several different kinds of frames in addition to the two identified in the example above. Getting a sense for the most appropriate frame will help you properly pitch the message. There are some common negotiation frames. Below is a chart of those frames and some questions that you can ask yourself before choosing that frame.

Frame	Question
Outcome	Is your counterpart concerned with a very specific outcome? Does he steer conversations towards his predetermined outcome?

Frame	Question
Altruistic	Are you and your counterpart having a more aspirational conversation about all the things that you two could accomplish if your companies were to align? Do you talk about more about possibilities and less about day-to-day details?
Identity	Is your counterpart's identity (role in the company, title, mission) wrapped up in a solution, or causing an impasse? Is he overly identified with his role or title in the company and will not agree to something that doesn't fit his sense of what the identity should do?
Process	Is your counterpart concerned about following all the steps in an established process? Do you find yourself discussing and negotiating aspects of the process of reaching an agreement to ensure that it is a fair process for everyone involved?
Loss/Gain	Is the negotiation being characterized as a win/win, or as a winner-take-all? (Look beyond the cliché's to what is really being asked of one another. I find that people say win/win and act as winner-take-all.)

Framing your conversation in the wrong frame can have unintended consequences. You cannot have an aspirational conversation with someone whose job it is to ensure that the buying process is fair. Your message of possibilities will not resonate with a purchaser as it would with the alliance manager. Therefore, you have a more aspirational conversation with the alliance manager and a more process oriented conversation with the purchasing department.

Because frames are very different from one another, the frame you choose for your message will have a tremendous impact on the course you take to reach a desired outcome. As a skilled negotiator, it is your job to recognize and select the appropriate frame for each conversation.

This chapter summarizes different aspects of influencing through messaging. Managing your message in these three ways, managing the content, actively listening, and framing the message is the easiest way to increase your influence. You have control over how you state something, how you listen to your counterpart, and how you frame your message. It is your responsibility as a skillful negotiator to control the messages that you send to your counterpart. Influential negotiators know that an attractive message is much more likely to be well received by their counterpart, enhancing their ability to easily reach favorable agreements.

Furthermore, you can influence your counterpart by really listing to them. People just want to be heard. No one really listens anymore. So many of us multitask that we miss half of what is said. Just taking the time to understand your counterpart will make you influential. Finally, take control of the

Successful negotiators choose to frame the issue in a way that will allow their counterpart to better hear the issue.

message by choosing an appropriate frame. Your message will be more easily received if it is framed appropriately and in a way that your counterpart can understand.

Influence encompasses the tools and actions you choose in order to subtly exert power to persuade. It is an effective and collaborative way to get people to change positions, attitudes and beliefs so that both of you can achieve the common goal of reaching a favorable agreement.

Chapter Ten

························▶

Negotiation Strategy

A randomly chosen set of tactics is not a negotiation strategy. Setting a deadline, offering a lowball number, and walking away in a huff are all examples of negotiation tactics. Singly, these tactics don't constitute a strategy. As a group, these tactics may be part of a larger strategy. A negotiation strategy answers the question, "how will I reach an agreement?" It is a plan of action that charts the overall course of the negotiation from the first interaction to the last conversation. A strategy brings tactics, tradeoffs, leverage points and the exchange of information into one cohesive plan in order to meet your business goals.

Successful negotiators create and follow a negotiation strategy. They actively decide where they are headed and pro-actively choose the methods for reaching their goals. (I call this a roadmap strategy.) They are more in control of the negotiation than their unsuccessful counterparts. They also stay on course when circumstances change, people change or new

Strategies provide direction for your negotiation team to achieve your company's goals at the bargaining table.

information demands a change in direction. Successful negotiators also take advantage of meetings and telephone conferences to continually move the negotiations along. (I call this a situational strategy.) They don't just go with the flow or talk just to hear the sound of their own voice. Although, I knew one attorney who was the master of talking for ten minutes without ever actually saying anything. She was brought into settlement conferences to buy time. Because successful negotiators are in control, they are more likely to meet their company's goals at the bargaining table.

Many negotiators don't develop strategies. Instead, they act like rudderless ships on the open sea bobbing from one current to the next during the entire negotiation process. I've seen negotiators react to whatever is happening at the time without giving thought to how they plan to achieve their business goals. Moreover, unsuccessful negotiators randomly choose tactics based on what has "worked" for them in the past, or based on what their colleagues think will work. Tactics support your strategy, yet these unsuccessful negotiators talk as if the tactics were the strategy.

In addition to creating a master strategy for the overall negotiation process, successful negotiators create strategies for individual meetings, phone calls and other more minor events. By far the biggest mistake that almost every negotiator makes is not creating a specific strategy for important meetings, conversations and information exchanges. Many of the negotiators that I've met, just show up for the meeting, the teleconference call, or they email the information to the other side without giving thought to how this particular interaction furthers their negotiation strategy. They don't consider how this interaction will help them accomplish their goals, or conversely, hinder them from achieving their goals. They might have some rough ideas in their head. Mostly they are ready to react to their counterpart, not actually taking an active role in creating their desired outcome.

I see this last mistake most acutely during mediation sessions. Often, neither the parties nor their attorneys come prepared with a strategy for the mediation session, which after all, is a negotiation session aimed at reaching an agreement. Attorneys prepare briefs that outline their positions and their interpretations of important case law. However, I rarely see evidence of any strategy in place for the negotiations. I usually see a go-with-the-flow

By far the biggest mistake that almost every negotiator makes is not creating a specific strategy for important meetings, conversations and information exchanges.

attitude during the back and forth conversations. On occasion I prepare people for mediation sessions and one of the things that I help them create is a negotiation strategy for the mediation session.

After reading this chapter you will have an understanding and appreciation for the importance of having clear negotiation strategies. This chapter will help you accomplish three things. First, you will have an appreciation for the importance of goal setting during the bargaining process. Second, you will understand the difference between a roadmap strategy and a situational strategy, and how the situational strategy supports your roadmap strategy. Third, you will also have read two real life stories in which the negotiators had clear, workable negotiation strategies. The people who came up with these strategies worked at small companies and had excellent negotiation skills.

A negotiation strategy answers the question, "how will I reach an agreement?" It is nearly impossible to create an effective negotiation strategy without having first set some clear negotiation goals. Before you create your roadmap strategy, establish some goals following these three guidelines.

Goal Setting at the Bargaining Table

A goal should be objectively reasonable, directly related to your underlying motivations for negotiating an agreement, and specific. An objectively reasonable goal is one in which an outsider — who has knowledge of your industry — would agree is obtainable under the circumstances. In other words, would an industry expert under the same set of circumstances agree that your goal is reasonable? Using office space as an example, I might want to pay $10 per square foot in a class A building in downtown Seattle, but any commercial broker I talk to would tell me that that number is not reasonable. It would, therefore, fail to meet the first element of a good negotiation goal.

A negotiation strategy answers the question, *"how will I reach an agreement?"*

On its face, the negotiation goal must be directly related to both your interests for negotiating an agreement and your business goals. It goes without saying that it is fruitless to set a goal that does not further your underlying motivations for negotiating and your business goals. Specificity is the final element in setting negotiation goals. I hear goals that are reasonable, related to my clients interests, but are vague. My clients say that they want a good deal. What does a "good deal" look like? Can you quantify it even more and set a percentage increase in business, or profit?

Choosing and Creating Strategies

Once you've established a goal, it is now time to consider your strategy. A strategy is a plan that charts the overall course of the negotiation from the first interaction to the last conversation. A strategy brings tactics, tradeoffs, leverage points and the exchange of information into one cohesive plan. It is also wise to anticipate roadblocks, your counterpart's positions and their likely tactics when creating your strategy.

Because a negotiation strategy supports your company's larger business goals, you must consider developing two kinds of strategies. A roadmap strategy charts the overall course for the negotiation, while a situational strategy helps you leverage a certain conversation or interaction in furtherance of your goals.

I recognized that I had a bifurcated way of looking at negotiation strategies when I started mediating cases. I knew from my experience as a trial lawyer that I should have an overall strategy for the case. I also knew from experience that I ought to develop a strategy for each hearing. I naturally brought that way of thinking to my mediation work. To my surprise, parties and attorneys did not appear to have a strategy for the mediation session, even though their case was likely to settle before going to trial. Developing a strategy for settling the case at mediation is an example of a situational strategy.

Roadmap Strategy

A roadmap strategy provides you, as the negotiator, a direction on how to best achieve your business goals at the bargaining table. To develop a roadmap strategy start by outlining any business purposes your company has for entering into the negotiation. Your outline should include your company's motivating factors for wanting to do business with the other company, the other company's motivating factors for doing business with you, and an honest analysis of your alternatives to negotiating. You want to know before you start negotiations if there are better alternatives to meeting your company's goals than engaging in negotiations with your counterpart.

The second element to this strategy is to develop a

straightforward method for negotiating that includes appropriate tactics, using your leverage, the right team players and the resources needed to accomplish your negotiation goals. I am often amazed that companies fail to look carefully at the second element to a roadmap strategy. I often see *ad hoc* negotiation teams that don't have the information or support they need to accomplish their goals. Not only should you have an idea of which tactics would support your strategy, you must also have the people with the right information and authority involved as well.

There are three generic strategic approaches. These approaches help give shape to your negotiation strategy.

Approach	Downside	Upside
Distributive (dividing a fixed resource)	Win-lose atmosphere Us versus them position Superiority versus inferiority tactics Perpetuates power imbalances	Quick and focused Useful for tight deadlines Bottom line driven when all things are really equal

Approach	Downside	Upside
Problem solving (consultative selling approach)	Drawn out conversations with no end in sight Lose focus and go off on a tangent Everyone thinks there should be unanimity to reach an agreement	Strong business relationships Minimize power plays See and solve big picture issues before they become a problem
Accommodating	One side concedes to reach an agreement Creates expectation of concessions in future negotiations Creates power imbalance where there was not one before	Brings harmony to business dealings Preserve important vendor/customer relationships (such as sole supplier relationships) Can create an obligation of reciprocity

To illustrate these concepts, let's look at a company entering into a negotiation with a larger company. In this example, the company had options as to which tactics to choose, which tradeoffs to make and how to use its leverage.

A start-up company developed a software product aimed at helping a specific segment of the population. It hoped to reach 25% of that population. A large software company was interested in integrating the start up's software into one of their existing web applications.

The start-up company's goals were: Integration of the new software application into the existing web application, exchanging information back and forth between the start up and the large company to improve and update the start up company's software, and a long term licensing agreement with the large company.

The start-up company's negotiation strategy was to develop a close working relationship based on a problem solving approach. Therefore, it would choose tactics that would support not only the problem solving approach, but also help them further their business goal of reaching 25% of a particular population.

Cultivating a champion would be one tactic that would support this strategy. A champion is someone not necessarily directly involved in the negotiations, but who is knowledgeable enough about the situation to help you along by speaking for you when you are not physically present for planning meetings that directly address your company. By cultivating a champion, the start up would get a virtual seat during conversations that they are not actually invited to attend. Further the champion might also lay the ground work for some future meetings, or explain the large company culture.

The start-up company would also choose tradeoffs to further their goals. One tradeoff might be exchanging the promise of a long term licensing agreement for a lower annual fee. Licensing the software for three years rather than one year would improve the start-up company's ability to improve software features and invest in enhancements.

Finally, this start-up company had leverage with the larger company. It created a product that would help an underserved segment of the population. Additionally, this segment of the population was attractive to advertisers because they have money to spend. The start-up company would weave this leverage into conversations with the larger company in order to establish its value to the company as a partner rather than as a mere vendor of software.

A randomly chosen set of tactics is not a negotiation strategy.

This example illustrates how important your roadmap strategy is to a successful negotiation. Without having thought this out in advance, the start up company would have been less likely to actually create a problem solving relationship between itself and the larger company. Without that type of relationship, the start up company would not have gotten the feedback it needed for continual improvements.

Finally, this example shows the relationship between the negotiation strategy and the company's plan to achieve its business goals. Similarly, a situational strategy supports your roadmap strategy in the same way that the roadmap strategy supports your business goals. A situational strategy does not detract from your overall strategy. It is a one-minute game plan for a particular conversation or interaction.

Situational Strategy

My experience with negotiators is that very few think to have a strategy for a particular conversation. In fact, most just wing-it, with disastrous results. I see this most clearly when the negotiations are contentious. It's almost as if the mere fact of being at odds necessitated a shoot from the hip attitude. It is unfortunate because it is precisely at times like those that negotiators have to keep their wits about them. Having a situational strategy in place during these sorts of conversations ensures that you will not only keep your temper, it also contributes to keeping the negotiations on track for your company as the other side will see that they cannot ruffle your feathers.

When developing a situational strategy, determine where you are in the process, who you are negotiating with from the other side, and what you need to accomplish from that particular conversation. For example, assume that your customer emailed you to tell you that they need a price concession. A situational strategy might be to call the purchasing agent who sent you the email to ask a specific set of questions about the need for the price concession without agreeing to make the reduction. This strategy would support your company's overall strategy of not permitting any more price reductions without making a thoughtful and targeted response.

A few years ago, a manufacturing company participated in a negotiation skills training session with me. One of the negotiator's explained their roadmap and situational strategy with a particular customer to me. It was a clear and effective strategy.

After being acquired by a larger corporate entity, the manufacturer set out to establish more aggressive business goals with their customers. The new corporate strategy was to develop deeper market strength by providing a more tightly knit product line to only a few key customers. However, one customer became increasingly unhappy with the company's performance on an array of issues.

The negotiation roadmap strategy for this customer and other key customers was to deepen those customer relationships. The manufacturer hoped to have a more collaborative relationship with their customers rather than that of a vendor on a long list of preferred vendors. The relationships that existed before the acquisition needed to be revisited now that the company was part of a larger corporate entity with a significant presence in the industry.

My experience with negotiators is that very few think to have a strategy for a particular conversation.

Because the negotiation team wanted to deepen relationships and because the customer had become dissatisfied with them, the team devised a situational negotiation strategy. They invited representatives from the customer's purchasing and engineering teams to the manufacturer's headquarters for a day long meeting. Once the customer accepted the invitation, the manufacturer decided it needed to do two things at this in-person meeting: Accept responsibility for their recent mistakes and explain the changes they were making to improve its product line.

The manufacturer's team knew that they had some pretty compelling positive leverage with the customer, despite the transitional screw ups. They had near perfect on-time delivery of their component parts, technological innovation and production flexibility. They also knew what tactics they wanted to use to support the situational and roadmap strategies, including offering on-site meetings where the customer could continue to evaluate the production line. Being at the plant helped create an openness with respect to their manufacturing processes.

This is a perfect example of how the overall business goals drove the negotiation strategy and how, by giving some thought and planning to developing situational strategy, an otherwise unpleasant customer relationship could be transformed, one thoughtful conversation at a time.

Strategies provide direction for your negotiation team to achieve your company's goals at the bargaining table. They encompass an approach that meets specific business goals, anticipates barriers and incorporates appropriate tactics. Strategies also allow multiple team members to work together while each plays their own part in the process.

Successful strategies allow you to effortlessly attain your goals. Take time to connect your roadmap strategy to your business goals. As the examples above show, having a negotiation strategy will help your company further its business goals.

Chapter Eleven

.....................................▶

Selecting and Managing Tactics

Negotiation tactics are simply the means you choose to achieve a specific goal. They are not the goal in themselves, nor are they to be confused with having a strategy. Negotiating tactics are the most widely discussed part of the negotiation process, and people talk out of both sides of their mouth about tactics. They brag about successfully using specific tactics, while they simultaneously complain about their counterpart's tactics. Tactics are definitely part of the gamesmanship of any negotiation.

Negotiation tactics come in many varieties and take on many forms. There are tactics that can be seen as positive and many more that are seen as negative. Because tactics help you achieve your goals, successful negotiators spend time considering and choosing tactics. They realize that there are many factors at play in any given negotiation and choosing wisely helps to ensure a favorable outcome.

Less successful negotiators, on the other hand, tend to react to situations, spending little time actively choosing tactics. As a result, conversations go off

Tactics are not a substitute for a negotiation strategy.

on tangents, things "get personal", negotiators engage in one-upmanship, and negotiations become derailed. For example, I sat across the bargaining table from a senior vice-president from a large company who started the conversation off by glaring at my colleague while asking an antagonizing question. That tactic was meant to put us on edge. Rather than having the intended effect of making us more malleable, it made us mad, and we pushed back by walking away. His choice in tactic was not too smart from my perspective.

My work training hundreds of negotiators led me to three conclusions. One, as a successful negotiator it is imperative that you recognize tactics so you are not drawn into reactionary conversations. Two, you need to choose tactics based on what you want to accomplish, your personality and that of your counterpart. Third, you need to categorize tactics based on one objective criteria: "Does it get me closer to my stated goal?" If it doesn't, don't use it.

By reading this chapter, you will have a method for characterizing tactics so you choose only those that will have the intended impact. You will also better manage tactics, which will allow you to make choices about how to respond to your counterpart. In the end, you will be far more effective and less reactive if you learn to recognize and manage tactics.

Types of Tactics
Broadly speaking, tactics must get you closer to your stated goal. If your stated goal is to win the business no matter what, you will choose one set of tactics. If your goal is to establish a long term supplier relationship, you will choose other tactics. By using this benchmark–does it get me closer to my stated goal–you can start to categorize tactics. I see three general categories of tactics: bad, neutral and good.

Bad Tactics. Bad tactics are those that don't get you any closer to your stated goal and don't further your negotiation strategy. Bad tactics actively create obstacles to agreements. Some examples of tactics that will not get you closer to your stated goal include stonewalling, attacking the person or being intentionally deceptive. While any tactic when taken to an extreme can become a bad tactic, rarely have I seen these examples result in a positive outcome. More usually, these tactics prevent the problem solving, brainstorming process.

Neutral Tactics. Neutral tactics are any tactic that can cut both ways depending on the situation and whether you are on the giving or receiving end. Sometimes a tactic will get you closer to your stated goal, sometimes it can backfire. I consider setting deadlines neutral. A deadline can be a very positive tactic when negotiations must legitimately come to a close. With everyone working to come to an agreement, negotiations can be efficient and effective, rather than a drain on resources.

A deadline can also trigger a negative response. I've seen two things happen. At a mediation session, I witnessed a party pull back from the bargaining table because he saw the deadline as a way to force him into a decision he was not ready to make. Think of those times that sales people told you that you have only minutes left to take advantage of an offer. If you're not ready to decide, no amount of time pressure will induce you to buy. Second, a client failed to enforce the deadline it set. Once that happened, their efforts to re-set deadlines were disregarded by their counterpart.

Good Tactics. Good tactics are those that get you closer to your stated goals and further your strategy. Just about all tactics can be considered good when they help you achieve your goal. In fact, I've been told by business people who've raised voices, slammed doors, and made threats that these tactics got the deal closed. I am dubious that the situation was as rosy as they reported. I know from my mediation experience that people have big egos and when the ego is hurt, people will find ways to even the score. Maybe not overtly, but they'll find a way to get even.

Categorizing Tactics

All tactics can be categorized depending on the situation, the personalities involved and the stated goals. At workshops and in coaching sessions, I ask negotiators to categorize the tactics they've used. Here are some examples from those sessions.

Bad Didn't work	Neutral Sometimes it worked	Good Always worked
Pile on requirements at the last minute	Double back to issue that you said was resolved	Changing the scene (going for coffee or lunch)
Name dropping	Continue talking until the situation is resolved	Offering incentives
Intimidation		Silence
Threats	Good Cop/Bad Cop	Allow the situation to "marinate"
Exaggerate the impact	Pretending to be ignorant of the situation	Disengage because it is not my battle to fight
Take the situation up to superiors for an answer	Respond at the last minute	Use either/or language
Give in early	Use time to wear the other side down	Take deal to a colleague for a second opinion
Pretend that you're not interested		

As you can see, categorization is subjective. Yet, the categories themselves are not. The one question that you need always ask yourself is this: "Will this get me closer to my stated goal?" If it does, it is a good tactic. If you're not sure, it is neutral. If you know that it will not, then don't use it. In the end you must actively choose your tactics wisely.

At one negotiation, my client and I actively chose the good cop/bad cop tactic. I was the bad cop. I said "no" a lot. My client's reasoning was that they were left with the relationship after the deal was negotiated, so they wanted to look like the reasonable one going forward. By actively choosing this tactic, my client was prepared for any negative fall out, such as complaints about my behavior or threats to leave the bargaining table. Now that you've taken time to think about which tactics will get you closer to your stated goal, you need to be prepared to manage your counterpart's tactics.

Managing Your Opponents Tactics

The single most important thing that you can do is recognize a tactic as a tactic. I scour the web looking for negotiation articles and I find dozens that give tips on what tactics to use in certain circumstances.

In one such article, an author gave purchasing agents advice to threaten to use a supplier's competitor. The author noted that suppliers will concede price rather than risk losing a customer. In other words, the threat is a tactic. The purchasing agent may have no intention to use your competitor; he is hoping that you'll cave before it gets that far.

It is imperative that you recognize tactics so you are not drawn into reactionary conversations.

The question that I use in these circumstances is this: "Is

it true?" Is it true that the customer needs a better price from your company? Is it true that your counterpart is the nice guy and you don't want to talk to his boss, because his boss has a temper? Is it true that the proposal has to be emailed by the 5 pm on Friday or they won't consider it? Maybe these statements are true and maybe they are not. The point is that you must test your assumptions and restrain yourself from reacting to the tactic. The tactic's power rests in your succumbing to it. If your counterpart slams out of the room and you hold the line and calmly pack your bag, the tactic is not effective. If you get weak in the knees and give in, it is effective. Ultimately, it is your choice to respond. Make a good choice.

The single most important thing that you can do is recognize a tactic is just a tactic.

Hardball Tactics. By far the most difficult situations are those in which your counterpart uses hardball tactics. I consider bullying, name calling, yelling, and lying hardball tactics. These tactics erode trust and undermine the relationship between the negotiators and their companies. Unfortunately, I see these tactics all too often and usually with disastrous results.

When faced with what you perceive as a hardball tactic, the best policy is to clearly name the tactic. To name the tactic means stating what you heard in the form of a neutral observation. For example you might say, "That statement sounds like a personal attack." By stating the behavior as an observation, you lessen the risk of escalating the conversation into a tit-for-tat. Bullies, who are most likely to use name calling as a tactic, put you on the defensive. You then lose focus on the issues at hand. A client used silence when faced with a professional buyer who attacked his integrity. The buyer recanted the statement after an awkward couple of minutes.

Bluffing. Dealing with bluffing at the bargaining table is difficult. A bluff is by its nature a fact, opinion or statement that you cannot verify. Bluffing is considered by just about everyone a completely natural part of the bargaining process, yet the line between a bluff and an out right lie can be blurry. From my perspective as an attorney, the line is drawn at fraud, which is loosely defined as a knowing deceit used to induce the other party into an agreement that he would not have made had it not been for the deceitful statement. In ordinary negotiations, bluffing can take many forms, from denying information to telling little white lies.

There are a couple of ways to detect bluffs or little white lies. First, carefully listen for mismatches between words spoken today and statements made in the past. Thankfully, most people are terrible liars and will unwittingly give you verbal clues that they are using a tactic. If you are face to face, carefully observe facial expressions, tone of voice and body language. Sometimes, these can be very obvious. I once observed a man tell me with a clenched fist that he was not mad at my client. Baloney! By far the most effective method for detecting bluffs is to thoroughly prepare. Knowing as much as you can throughout the negotiation, including debriefing with colleagues if there are multiple points of contact, will give you the upper hand to head a bluff off at the pass.

Successful negotiators recognize that tactics are the means to an end; not the end in and of themselves. They know it is their responsibility to carefully select the tactics they use and to only pick those that help them achieve their goals. By controlling their choice of tactics, they are not blindly entering into any negotiation. Nor do successful negotiators use the same tactics in every situation. They recognize that what

A bluff is a fact, opinion or statement that you cannot verify.

121

worked for them last time might explode on them this time. They also recognize tactics are just tactics, and don't take them so personally.

You have two responsibilities with respect to tactics. You have to choose tactics to meet your goals and you have to recognize and manage your counterpart's tactics. Ultimately, you are choosing to take an active role in the back and forth process, and by doing so, you will be more effective and less reactive at the bargaining table.

Chapter Twelve

··▶

Planning

Preparation is essential to success at the bargaining table because — unlike the rest of the negotiation process — it is 100% within your control. You cannot control your counterpart, her reactions, her negotiation or conflict style. Nor can you control what information your counterpart will share or hide from you. You, on the other hand, can control your reactions, share appropriate information, and anticipate potential obstacles by being fully prepared for the negotiation.

General Eisenhower was said to have quipped, "Plans are nothing, planning is everything." Successful negotiators plan for negotiation session not because the planning will ensure that the session will go as planned, but because planning activities ensure that the negotiator is prepared for any thing that might arise. In considering several different aspects of an upcoming negotiation, successful negotiators will often uncover assumptions that they are making, anticipate obstacles to reaching an agreement or discover different ways

Planning and preparation are within your control so make sure you are ready for all of your negotiation conversations.

of reaching their company's goals.

Unsuccessful negotiators often don't plan and they have some consistent excuses for not planning. They don't set aside time, claiming that they don't have the time in the day to think about the negotiation. Even if they did have the time, they don't know what they should be considering. And, if they did have the time, and they did know what they should consider, things change and so what difference does it make any way, because they will wing-it.

Several of my clients have achieved spectacular success at the bargaining table as a result of actively preparing for negotiation sessions. Some have gotten more money from the deal, others have found alternative means to meet company goals, while others have developed solid relationships with their customers. These are all factors to your success as a business, and they are factors to your success as a negotiator.

I purposefully placed this chapter last because my experience as an adjunct professor proved unsuccessful negotiators have a hard time planning when concepts like leverage or influence are not fully understood. Because the class had the luxury of ten weeks of study, they could break negotiations into segments and thus learn how to plan as they moved through the material rather than all at once. Because many of you won't have that same luxury, you may choose to start here. If you are reading this chapter first, I urge you to consult individual chapters if you don't understand the concept that I am referring to.

Continually use this chapter as a guide regardless of whether you are reading this chapter first or after reading all of the other chapters. After reading the following paragraphs describing planning activities, answer the questions presented in the Best Practices section in the order that they are presented. I added sample answers so you can get an idea of what a planning session might reveal to you. My aim is to

have you prepare on your own as you and I would prepare if we were working together. I am always looking for patterns, connections or an advantage at the bargaining table. Often, leverage points or other advantages will reveal themselves as you consider other elements of the negotiation process.

Confession

I have a confession to make—I listened in on someone else's conversation at a Starbucks. In fact, I listed as two lawyers, who I am guessing worked as in-house counsel for one of the large Seattle based corporations, complained about a particular negotiation. What's more, I was so happy to listen to them, that I was delighted to get a text message that my colleague was running late. I listened to them with my negotiation coaches' hat on. Here was the rhythm. #1 Guy started by asking #2 Guy what their next move should be at the bargaining table. #2 Guy complained about the personality of their counterpart. #1 Guy agreed and added a few words. #2 Guy added that their counterpart's requests were unreasonable. #1 Guy agreed and complained again about their counterpart's personality. And on it went for 15 minutes. Then they left.

Planning is more than a b.s. session at a local Starbucks. Ok, maybe they were blowing off steam, but even when my clients blow off steam with me, we look for hidden motivations, bad tactics, or wrong assumptions. We do way more than just complain that the person's personality could use improvement or that their positions are unreasonable. I want to know what is DRIVING the behavior, position or tactic. Getting

Research and planning can rid us of many assumptions— and the resulting problems—that we face in a negotiation.

to the bottom of those issues will prove to be worth your while at the bargaining session. If you have only a few minutes to plan what should you do or think about?

Thoughts on Preparation

Here are some ideas about steps to take in order to prepare before your next negotiation session. Start by looking at what you want and why you want it. What are your company's goals? Are they specific and objectively justifiable? How do these goals fit in with your larger business strategy? Next, look at your alternatives to negotiating. Is there a better way to meet your goals other than by negotiating with your counterpart?

Then gather your independent information, whether it is about the market place or about the customer or your competitors. Now, using any information that you have at your fingertips, list your interests or what motivates you to negotiate? Next, imagine what might be motivating them to negotiate. Step into their shoes for a moment. This is crucial because studies show that successful negotiators spend more time thinking about what the other party's interests might be than do less skilled and less successful negotiators.

Because relationships play a large part in negotiations, understand the nature of the relationship with the customer before you start any conversations.

Now, look at your trade-offs and your leverage points. You should start to see some patterns, connections, and common ground. A strategy may even present itself. Select appropriate tactics to support your strategy. Don't forget to know your walk away point. Not the bluffing walk away point when you know that you will go back to the table,

but the real walk away point at which is does not make financial sense to stay in this negotiation. All of these steps support and are connected to your original business goal for entering the negotiation in the first place.

There are some other considerations too. Factor in all the people you may have conversations with from purchasing to engineering. What are their roles at the bargaining table? Are there any other parties that should be at the table? Finally, the most important consideration is the relationship you have with the other person and the company they represent. Because relationships play a large part in negotiations, understand the nature of the relationship with the customer before you start any conversations. The more important the relationship, the more time you need to prepare to ensure that the negotiation process does not damage the relationship.

One final note, research and planning can rid us of many assumptions — and the resulting problems — that we face in a negotiation. If we do not have adequate information, we are likely to make assumptions. Assumptions are extremely dangerous because when we do not know something, we will fill in the blank with the first thing that enters our mind. My experience as a trial attorney taught me that people will fill in any informational gaps with what ever comes to mind, and it might not be a proven fact. Accurate information is the most valuable asset you can have, so get plenty of it.

Planning Best Practices

To avoid anchoring the entire negotiation process to your counterpart's hidden motives and stated positions start by working through the following three steps in order. I urge you to start any planning process by first looking at the negotiation from your point of view. Too often I see companies derail themselves by focusing too much on their counterpart and forgetting about what they need, want and — more importantly — what they have to have.

Within the three steps outlined below, I've included questions I've used with clients in coaching and strategic planning sessions.[1] This is not an exhaustive list, nor may this list be appropriate for your negotiations. The questions that follow, though, are designed to help you understand that planning is a process of putting seemingly different parts together into one coherent package.

In order to give some life to the steps and the questions, I created a fictional client and fictional, sample answers to my planning questions. Imagine as you read this that the fictional client is a sales representative at a small manufacturing company. Her company sells only one product to ABC Co via multi-year supplier agreement. This year ABC Co wants to re-negotiate the price of the widget with her company, but many of the other terms of the deal will stay the same. Her sample answers to my questions are in italics.

Step One – From Your Company's Point of View

Looking at the negotiations from your company's point of view, how would you answer these questions?

Concept	Questions	Sample Answers
Goals	What business goals are you trying to achieve? How does the anticipated agreement meet those goals?	Increase total sales volume by 20% to five of our most important customers. A favorable agreement with ABC Co. would give our company a 2% increase in price over 3 years, and a 5% increase in volume over the next 12 months, with meetings in year 2 and 3 to anticipate purchase volumes.

Concept	Questions	Sample Answers
Motivations	What are your interests or motivations at the bargaining table? (These should support your business goals.) What motivations are you comfortable revealing? Which ones will you not reveal?	Develop a more collaborative supplier/ customer relationship by talking with all of the customer's negotiators, get clearer forecasting methods from customer in place so we can keep our inventory of raw materials at a minimum, negotiate minimal price increases based on the increased cost of raw materials, etc. Reveal -collaboration and price for raw materials. Not reveal – our margins depending on how much of the customer's inventory we have on hand at any given moment.

Concept	Questions	Sample Answers
Assumptions	List any assumptions you have for this negotiation. (Like, price will be an issue, or that you will be negotiating only with a purchasing representative.) What questions will you ask your counterpart to make sure that these assumptions are valid?	I assume that the purchasing department will want a price decrease over the next 3 years. I think that the engineers will want to make changes to our products that could cost us money if we don't include design changes in the price per widget. I assume that the customer will want to negotiate this deal over email. What changes would you like to see in the new contract? What design changes do you anticipate needing to make to your product over the next 3 years? What do you see has the next 2 or 3 steps in the process?
Common Ground	From your perspective, what concerns, needs, wants might you and your counterpart share. (For example, you both may want flexibility, but how you both define flexibility could be at odds.)	Accurate forecasting, keeping prices for raw materials in check, accurate just-in-time shipping and delivery.

Concept	Questions	Sample Answers
Negotiating Money	What is your bottom line cost for this product? (Remember, this figure is not the bluff, walk away point, but the point at which is just doesn't make financial sense to continue with the negotiations.)	Our bottom line would be $12.50 per widget at an agreed to volume of no less than 10,000 widgets per month over the course of the next 12 months. Anything less than that and we are losing money.
	What range would you like to agree within?	$12.70 to $12.95 per widget. Our target it $12.75.
	What information do you have about your counterpart's budget range?	The current contract price that will expire at the end of this month is $12.63 per widget. They will not likely agree to more than $12.95 per widget and may even want to pay as little as $12.60 per widget.

Concept	Questions	Sample Answers
Alternatives	What alternative methods or paths do you have to meet your company's business goals How realistic are your alternatives?	Shift business away from ABC Co and solicit more business from XYZ Co. XYZ Co tell us that they are not happy with their California supplier and would like to have another west coast vendor supply their Sacramento plant. They seem eager to move business to us no later than by the end of Q3. 50/50 chance. They could move the business to us but we may have some hidden costs associated with their business. We don't know enough yet.

Concept	Questions	Sample Answers
Tradeoffs	What would you be willing to give to the customer? What would you be willing to receive in exchange?	We would be willing to trade the type of shipping and delivery schedule, the warranty period, and price increase only if we were permitted to pass along raw commodity increases quarterly. Accurate monthly forecasts (i.e. within 500 widgets of monthly total), guaranteed quarterly purchase amounts, opportunity to bid on other products that we offer but that they don't purchase from us.

Concept	Questions	Sample Answers
Leverage	What do you have that is positive? What do you have that is negative? What do you have that is normative? (That is, what shared values do you have, or ways to leverage common ground.)	Existing product sales with 99% quality rating from ABC Co., great relationships with the engineers at ABC Co., ability to meet changes in demand (i.e. more this week, less for the next two weeks) with relative ease. We could walk away. Then they could use our competitor, but that competitor closed their west coast plant. They only have a Texas plant. If we could not agree to terms and price, it could mean a several month chink in the supply chain for ABC Co. to move their business to the competitor. We both want to serve the end user with a high quality, inexpensive widget. We both value innovations that keep the product cost effective while maintaining quality.

Concept	Questions	Sample Answers
Strategy	What approach should you take and why? Are there any meetings that you know of now that may require a specific strategy just for that meeting? What do you want to accomplish at that meeting? How will talking about new products or buying some existing products help you in the long run?	Problem solving. We want to work with them and not against them. We both achieve our goals by working a collaboratively as possible. We are trying to schedule a face-to-face meeting next month. I want to find out more information about any new products that ABC Co will roll out in the next 12 months. I want to talk about ABC purchasing other products from us for existing ABC products. Before the face-to-face, I need to talk to Craig at ABC Co engineering department for more info, if possible. We can only offer zero price increase if there is more volume. If increased volume is not possible, I will need to make sure we have at least a small price increase.

Concept	Questions	Sample Answers
Tactics	What tactics will you use to further your strategy and goals? Which tactics will you avoid?	Sharing information within reason. Asking open ended questions to define problems or areas of concern, willingness to be first to make tradeoff to start back and forth conversation. Good cop/Bad cop we got caught last time and looked foolish, threats to walk away unless their number is at or below $12.50 per widget.
My Negotiation Team	Who do you need to check in with during this negotiation? How should you all stay in the loop? Who could I bounce questions off of?	Pete, Regional VP sales, Tom in materials management, Tiffany customer service liaison for ABC Co. We all agreed to email each other when any one of us talks to ABC Co. Jeanette, she's dealt with them before.

Step Two – From Your Counterpart's Point of View

Now that you've looked at your company's goals, leverage and tradeoffs, you are prepared to analyze the negotiations from your counterpart's point of view. Looking at the negotiations from your counterpart's point of view, how would you answer these questions?

Concept	Questions	Sample Answers
Goals	What business goals do you think they are they trying to achieve? How does the anticipated agreement meet their goals?	Maintain diversity in supply chain, maintain discount pricing, and maintain high quality and on-time delivery of their end product to their customer. A favorable agreement with us would give them a steady supply of widgets from a great supplier with a reputation for quality and flexibility. We help them meet goals of quality, cost effective parts and on-time delivery.

Concept	Questions	Sample Answers
Motivations	What are their interests or motivations at the bargaining table? What hidden motivations might they have?	Develop a more cooperative supplier/ customer relationship within reason, not have their business rest on any one supplier, price effectiveness. Use competitors pricing against us to get us to lower our price, pass more risk to us by asking us to hold more inventory for them, get us to concede price without addressing problems they have with forecasting.

Concept	Questions	Sample Answers
Assumptions	List any assumptions you think that they might have for this negotiation. What do I need to tell them about these assumptions?	They think that we would be willing to cut our price to keep their business. They think that they can call the Regional VP to go over my head. They might expect us to raise our price because price was an issue last time too. Regional VP has given me authority to negotiate this deal and he will not be involved in the day-to-day negotiations. We are willing to make tradeoffs to keep the price competitive and are willing to look at a range of options to make that happen, but that we are not going to concede price because our cost for raw materials is up over this time last year.

Concept	Questions	Sample Answers
Common Ground	From your perspective, what concerns, needs, wants might you and your counterpart share from the agreement. (For example, you both may want to flexibility, but how you both define flexibility could be at odds.)	Accurate forecasting, keeping prices for raw materials in check, accurate just-in-time shipping and delivery.
Negotiating Money	What is the highest price that the customer would probably pay for your product? Where is their discomfort zone?	We guess it could be at about $12.95. We guess at about $12.85 per widget.
Alternatives	What alternative methods or paths do they have to meet their business goals? How realistic are their alternatives?	Shift business away from us to another supplier. It is not a quick and easy switch though. Our competitor closed their California plant and would have to supply ABC Co from Texas. But, I am not sure. They could already have things in place to make the switch.

Concept	Questions	Sample Answers
Tradeoffs	What do you think that they would most likely be willing to offer you as a tradeoff? What do you think about that tradeoff? If that is the case, then what do you want from them as a tradeoff?	Chance to be a part of the RFP process for the next generation of product that our widget would go into. It's only a bid and not the actual supplier contract, so not as valuable to us as better forecasting and a small price increase this year. We've been promised this before and then lost the contract. We really have to have better forecasting. That would make a big difference to our bottom line.
Leverage	What do they have that is positive? What do they have that is negative?	Existing contract that is fairly profitable for us. Opportunities for more product sales. Shifting business to our competitor. Using threats of competitors pricing to force us to lower our pricing.

Concept	Questions	Sample Answers
Strategy	What approach will they most likely take?	Distributive. It could be all about price. But, they've also said that they would like to be more collaborative with their top tier suppliers.
Tactics	What tactics will they likely use? How will you avoid falling into the trap their tactics might create?	Lowball offer on price, good cop/bad cop, going over my head, offering us the chance to be a part of the RFP, last minute decisions. Make sure that the Regional VP is in the loop, make sure the conversation is about tradeoffs, stop and think before answering any of their emails, talking to management about the chance to be a part of the RFP before I respond to that issue.

Concept	Questions	Sample Answers
Their Negotiation Team	Who is part of their team?	Sarah, lead purchasing. Maybe talk to Craig in engineering about new product launches at ABC Co in the near future. I don't know who Sarah reports to now. I will need to find that out.

Step Three – Continue to Track the Negotiations.

Negotiations are not static, so it is important to continue to track the progress of the negotiations against your company's business goals and against the value of the overall deal for both tangible and intangible terms. Because negotiations can happen over time and involve different people, be sure that you have some system in place — even just an email folder — to keep correspondence and notes. Some of my clients have faced huge shifts in strategy and tactics at the bargaining table. By having good notes from previous conversations and email exchanges, my clients avoided making concessions that they said earlier in the process they would not make.

Whenever possible start all conversations with shared interests or common ground.

One final note, whenever possible start all conversations with shared interests or common ground. It doesn't matter whether the conversation is about money or delivery schedules or personalities, start conversations with what your company and your counterpart's company want from the business relationship. I've used this technique with great success as a mediator and as an attorney representing my clients at the bargaining table. It works because it forces both of you to focus on the positive attributes and not solely on the negative.

Planning and preparation are within your control so make sure you are ready for all of your negotiation conversations. After awhile, you will start answering the questions listed in this chapter as a matter of habit and will ask your teammates these same questions. Before long, you will develop the skills and confidence necessary to consistently negotiate great deals.

References & Notes

........................▶

Chapter One

[1]Fisher, Roger, Ury, William, Patton, Bruce. *Getting to Yes: Negotiating Agreement without Giving In.* 2nd ed. New York: Penguin, 1991.

[2]Ury, William. *Getting Past No: Negotiating Your Way From Confrontation to Cooperation.* New York: Bantam, 1993.

Chapter Two

[1]Shell, G. Richard. *Bargaining for Advantage: Negotiation Strategies for Reasonable People.* 2nd ed. New York: Penguin, 2006.

[2]Ury, William. *Getting Past No: Negotiating Your Way From Confrontation to Cooperation.* New York: Bantam, 1993.

Chapter Three

[1]Ury, William. *Getting Past No: Negotiating Your Way From Confrontation to Cooperation.* New York: Bantam, 1993.

References & Notes

Chapter Four

[1]For free copies of these diagrams, visit the shopping cart at www.jnyden.com.

[2]Cost accounting is an art and a science so no company is ever perfect, but as a seller, the better you understand the true and full costs associated with your wares, the more effective negotiator you will be.

Chapter Five

[1]This section is based on the article, *The Fine Art of Making Concessions*. Deepak Malhotra. Negotiation. Project on Negotiation, vol.9, number 1, January 2006. This title further illustrates my point that people are using these very different terms interchangeably. Business people should keep the distinctions between tradeoffs and concessions clear in their own mind.

Chapter Seven

[1]Shell, G. Richard. *Bargaining for Advantage: Negotiation Strategies for Reasonable People*. 2nd ed. New York: Penguin, 2006.

[2]By viable I mean an alternative that is equal to your deal in every aspect from price, to delivery, to customer support. Most large businesses fall into the trap of thinking that all businesses are alike and that a deal with your company will be exactly like a deal with your competitor. My experience tells me that this is wrong on many levels.

[3]Shell, G. Richard. *Bargaining for Advantage: Negotiation Strategies for Reasonable People*. 2nd ed. New York: Penguin, 2006.

[4]Shell, G. Richard. *Bargaining for Advantage: Negotiation Strategies for Reasonable People*. 2nd ed. New York: Penguin, 2006.

[5]Shell, G. Richard. *Bargaining for Advantage: Negotiation Strategies for Reasonable People*. 2nd ed. New York: Penguin, 2006.

[6]Shell, G. Richard. *Bargaining for Advantage: Negotiation Strategies for Reasonable People*. 2nd ed. New York: Penguin, 2006.

References & Notes

Chapter Eight

[1]William Lincoln, founder and Executive Director of Conflict Resolution, Research and Resource Institute, Inc and Co-Director of the St. Petersburg-based Russian-American Program on Conflictology.

[2]*Are You Too Powerful For Your Own Good?* Ann Tenbrunsel. Negotiation. Project on Negotiation, vol. 8, number 9, September 2005.

Chapter 9

[1]Lweicki, Roy, David Saunders, and Bruce Barry. *Negotiation.* 5th ed. New York: McGraw-Hill, 2006.

Chapter Twelve

[1]For a free set of blank worksheets without the sample answers, visit the shopping cart at www.jnyden.com.

Bibliography

........................➤

Babcock, Linda and Laschever, Sara. *Women Don't Ask: Negotiation and the Gender Divide.* Princeton: Princeton University Press, 2003.

Camp, Jim. *Start With No: The Negotiation Tools That The Pros Don't Want You To Know.* New York: Crown Business, 2002.

Connolly, Mickey, Richard Rianoshek. *Communication Catalyst: The Fast (but not stupid) Track to Value for Customers, Investors and Employees.* Chicago: Dearborn, 2002.

Fisher, Roger, Ury, William and Patton, Bruce. *Getting to Yes: Negotiating Agreement Without Giving In.* Second Edition. New York: Penguin Press, 1991.

Kolb, Deborah M, Williams, Judith. *Everyday Negotiation: Navigating the Hidden Agenda in Bargaining.* San Francisco: Jossey-Bass, 2003.

Lweicki, Roy, David Saunders, and Bruce Barry. *Negotiation.* 5th ed. New York: McGraw-Hill, 2006.

Bibliography

Nierenberg, Gerard I. *The Complete Negotiator.* New York: Nierenberg & Zeif Publishers, 1986.

Patterson, Kerry, Joseph Grenny, Ron McMillan, Al Switzer. *CrucialConfrontations: Tools for Resolving Broken Promises, Violated Expectations,* and Bad Behavior. New York: McGraw Hill, 2005.

Patterson, Kerry, Joseph Grenny, Ron McMillan, Al Switzer. *Crucial Conversations: Tools for Talking When the Stakes are High.* New York: McGraw Hill, 2002.

Raiffa, Howard. *The Art and Science of Negotiation. How to Resolve Conflicts and Get the Best out of Bargaining.* Cambridge: Harvard University Press, 1982.

Scott, Susan. *Fierce Conversations: Achieving Success at Work and in Life, One Conversation at a Time.* New York: Viking, 2002.

Shell, G. Richard. *Bargaining for Advantage: Negotiation Strategies for Reasonable People.* 2nd ed. New York: Penguin, 2006.

Stone, Douglas, Bruce Patton, Sheila Heen. *Difficult Conversations: How to Discuss What Matters Most.* New York: Penguin, 1999.

Ury, William. *Getting Past No: Negotiating Your way From Confrontation to Cooperation.* New York: Bantam, 1993.

About The Author

Jeanette Nyden helps business people strike better deals by improving their confidence and skill level at the bargaining table. With Ms. Nyden's coaching and training, clients see immediate and recognizable performance improvement. Specifically, negotiators improve their communication techniques (even when dealing with difficult people), level an uneven playing field and increase their influence. Ms. Nyden leverages improvements in technology to offer virtual training and coaching as well as traditional, in-person training.

Recognizing in 2003 that business people needed relevant and practical negotiation advice, Ms. Nyden started J. Nyden & Co, Inc. Since then, Ms. Nyden has trained and coached hundreds of people at businesses ranging from powerhouses like Microsoft to start-ups like NetStar Communications. Ms. Nyden is an active, professional mediator, and an adjunct professor in Seattle, Washington.

Ms. Nyden earned her B.A. and Juris Doctorate from Southern Illinois University. Between 2003 and 2007, she donated hundreds of hours mediating disputes for the Pierce County Center for Dispute Resolution, a non-profit organization. Ms Nyden has lived with her husband in Seattle, Washington since 2002.

J.Nyden & Co.

..............................▶

**Everyone you work with—customers, vendors, contractors—
are demanding that you give them a better deal. Are you getting
the deals *you* want?**

J. Nyden & Co., helps business people strike better deals by
improving their confidence and skill level at the bargaining table.
Whether you are negotiating for the first time, or are a seasoned
professional, our coaching and training services will immediately
improve your skill level and your company's profitability. We work
with mid-market companies who negotiate complex contracts with
much larger organizations. We guarantee that our training and
coaching will be customized, practical and relevant to your needs.

Services Include
Negotiation Skills Assessment
Corporate Training and Coaching (virtual and in-person)
Keynote Presentations and Conference Break-Out Sessions
Meeting Facilitation/Mediation

For more information about our Negotiation Skills Assessment,
Coaching or Training programs, please contact us at:

Jeanette Nyden, J.D.
J. Nyden & Co., Inc.
5005 51st Ave S
Seattle, WA 98118
206-723-3472
info@jnyden.com
http://www.jnyden.com

Free worksheets associated to some of the chapters in this book
are available by visiting the website.

CPSIA information can be obtained at www.ICGtesting.com
Printed in the USA
265911BV00004B/19/P

9 780981 800479